25 CYCLE ROUTES

In and Around
GLASGOW

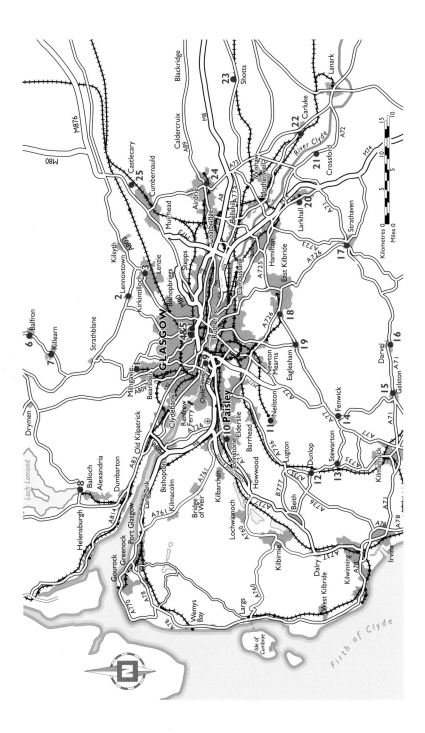

25 CYCLE ROUTES

In and Around
GLASGOW

Erl B. Wilkie

With a Foreword by the CTC

Strathclyde
ROADS
Caring for Life

EDINBURGH:HMSO

First published 1996

Applications for reproduction should be made to HMSO

Also available in this series: *25 Cycle Routes – Edinburgh and Lothian*

Acknowledgements

I wish to thank Strathclyde Regional Council Roads and Transportation Committee for agreeing to provide financial support for this book; the Director of Roads, Mr Donald Carruthers, for his support; Allan MacLean, a colleague of note, who supplied some photographs; and to Iain Robinson for the first-class maps. I would also like to thank the staff of the Mitchell Library, Glasgow, for their help in my research; to my friend, Donald Christie, for cycling some of the routes with me; and finally to Anne, my wife, and Kirsten, my daughter, for their support and understanding.

This book does not reflect the policy on cycling of any successor authority to Strathclyde Regional Council.

British Library Cataloguing in Publication Data

A catalogue record for this book is available from the British Library

ISBN 0 11 495718 5

CONTENTS

FOREWORD BY THE CTC

Cycling is healthy, environmentally-friendly – and above all fun! Travel at your own pace, meet people along the way and experience the real country. Explore parts of the country that you didn't know existed – and improve your fitness at the same time! Cycling is good for you, so go by bike, and you'll feel a whole lot better for it!

Safety considerations and equipment needed

- A few days before you plan to go cycling, check your bike thoroughly for broken, worn and/or loose parts. In particular, check for worn tyres and broken/loose spokes. Ensure that both brakes and the gear system are working well, with the chain lightly oiled and running smoothly. If in doubt, your local bike shop will be able to advise further. Better to fix anything now, than to spoil your cycle ride later! Low gears will be useful for any hills or strong winds.

- Carry a cycle lock and key and a small tool kit (spare inner tube, tyre levers, small adjustable spanner, puncture repair outfit, pump and allen keys if your bike needs them).

- If possible, luggage should be carried on the bike, not on your back, although you should be able to fit everything you need into an expanding bumbag. A rear carrying rack is useful. Ideally, pack everything into plastic bags inside a saddlebag or panniers, which are properly secured to this rack. Ensure that when "loaded" your luggage is well balanced, and that its weight doesn't affect your steering/handling of the bike. Check that nothing will fall into your wheels.

- Always carry food and water, for example sandwiches, biscuits and a full water bottle. Cyclists are advised to eat and drink "little and often".

- Comfortable clothing which allows freedom of movement is recommended, and for colder weather take warm clothing: two or three layers (a T-shirt and long-sleeved jerseys) are best. You can take off a layer or two once you've warmed-up and put them back on again if you stop or if it gets cold. Several layers allow precise

METRIC MEASUREMENTS

At the beginning of each route, the distance is given in miles and kilometres. Within the text, all measurements are metric for simplicity (and indeed our Ordnance Survey maps are now all metric). However, it was felt that a conversion table might be useful to those readers who, like the author, still tend to think in Imperial terms.

The basic statistic to remember is that one kilometre is five-eighths of a mile. Half a mile is equivalent to 800 metres and a quarter-mile is 400 metres. Below that distance, yards and metres are little different in practical terms.

km	miles
1	0.625
1.6	1
2	1.25
3	1.875
3.2	2
4	2.5
4.8	3
5	3.125
6	3.75
6.4	4
7	4.375
8	5
9	5.625
10	6.25
16	10

temperature control. It is also a good idea to carry wet-weather gear and/or a wind-proof garment if the weather looks as if it may turn bad. A peaked cap can help protect your eyes from rain and wind, helping you to see where you're going! For hot weather don't forget your sun cream and sunglasses!
You don't have to wear specialist cycling clothing to enjoy cycling – wear what you feel comfortable in. Padded shorts, gloves, cycling shoes, cycle helmets and much more can be purchased at cycle shops if you're interested. N.B. It is not compulsory to wear a helmet, and the choice is yours. The CTC can provide further information on helmets if needed.

- Check that your riding position is comfortable. Saddle height: when seated, place your heel on the pedal when it is at its lowest point. Your leg should be straight, and your knee just off the locked position. On the subject of riding comfort, many bikes are supplied with saddles designed for men (long and narrow). Women may prefer to use a woman's saddle (shorter and wider at the back). These are available from bike shops.

- There is some useful advice and information given for cyclists in the *Highway Code*. This is available from garages, bookshops and may be found in your library.

- If you think that you may be cycling when it is dark, you will need to fit front and rear lights (this is a legal requirement). Lights and reflectors/ reflective band/jacket are also useful in bad weather conditions.

- In the event of an accident, it is advisable to note the time and place of the incident, the names and addresses of those involved, details of their insurance company, any vehicle registration numbers and details of any witnesses present. In the event of injury or damage, report the accident to the police immediately.

- Some of the routes in this book use off-road paths which are shared with pedestrians. Please be courteous and friendly to people you meet and give way to walkers if necessary. A bicycle bell is useful for warning others of your approach.

For further information about cycling . . .

The CTC (Cyclist's Touring Club) is Britain's largest cycling organisation, and can provide a wealth of information and advice about all aspects of cycling. The CTC works on behalf of *all* cyclists to promote cycling and to protect cyclists' interests.

Join the CTC and enjoy *free* third-party insurance, legal aid, touring and technical information, a bi-monthly magazine and a cyclists' handbook. The CTC also organises an annual holiday programme, co-ordinates National Bike Week, runs a wide-ranging and effective network of cycle campaigners and holds weekly cycle rides all over the country.

For details of these, and our many other services, contact the CTC at: Cotterell House, 69 Meadrow, Godalming, Surrey GU7 3HS, or telephone 01483 417217, fax 01483 426994.

INTRODUCTION

This book contains 25 cycle routes around Glasgow covering a complete 360 degree radius around the city, with connections into the city at various locations. Each of the routes is interlinked *except Routes 9 and 25*, but even in these locations the routes are connected by two areas of linear, cycleable pathways. The routes vary in length from 14.5 km (9 miles) to 50 km (31 miles) and in difficulty from easy to very demanding. Owing to the geography of West Central Scotland it is impossible to find any length of totally flat terrain, therefore even the easiest routes in this book have small hilly stretches.

For the most part the routes use the network of minor roads, with negligible vehicular traffic flows, which are so abundant in this part of the world and therefore are ideal for cycling. Many of the routes also connect with, and use, lengths of the existing network of cycle routes or the Forth and Clyde Canal tow path. There is no particularly difficult surface to negotiate along these routes, although some short distances of off-road stretches can be muddy in wet weather and sometimes the path can be narrow.

It is completely legal to cycle on all of these routes in their entirety so no opposition to cycling should be encountered. There are one or two locations where to be absolutely on the safe side I have recommended that the cyclist dismount, but this is in the interest of safety or manoeuvrability not legality. On occasion some of the routes use A- and B-class roads for short distances but I have avoided using very busy roads and have only recommended a route along a stretch of A- or B-class road when I felt it was safe enough to do so. However readers must make their own judgement about safety depending on the circumstances prevailing at the time. If in doubt do not attempt it!

Where possible the routes start and finish at a railway station. If however, there is no railway in the vicinity of the route it starts at a convenient car park.

I hope you will enjoy these routes, which pass through a very varied terrain and which I feel show the area around Scotland's largest city at its scenic best.

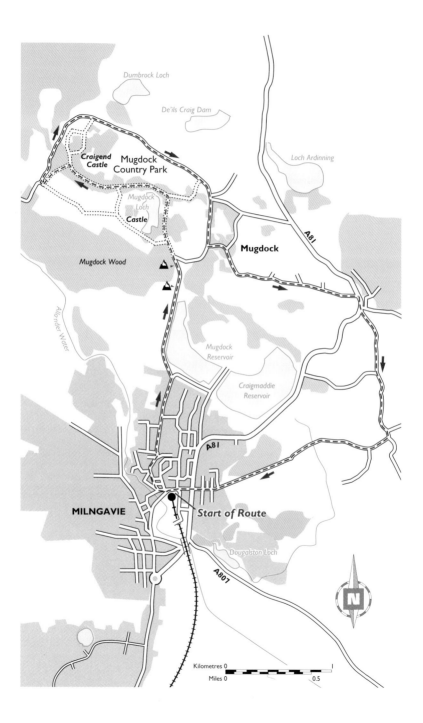

Dumbrock Loch

De'ils Craig Dam

Loch Ardinning

Craigend Castle Mugdock Country Park

Mugdock Loch

Castle

Mugdock Wood

Mugdock

Allander Water

A81

Mugdock Reservoir

Craigmaddie Reservoir

A81

MILNGAVIE

Start of Route

Dougalston Loch

A807

Kilometres 0 · · · · · · · · 1
Miles 0 · · · · 0.5

N

MILNGAVIE TO MUGDOCK COUNTRY PARK

Leave the car park at Milngavie Railway Station and turn left along Station Road for about 100 m, taking care along this stretch of busy dual carriageway, and turn right into Ellangowan Road, which later becomes Mugdock Road. If the reader is travelling by car to the beginning of the route, then there are convenient car parks adjacent to the junction of Station Road and Ellangowan Road.

Follow this road for just over 1.5 km climbing all the time, passing en route Mugdock and Craigmaddie Reservoirs, to where Mugdock Road makes a U-turn up a steep gradient. At this point the access road to Mugdock Country Park commences straight on, just as Mugdock Road begins its sharp turn, and continues for a short distance to South Lodge car park. The Mugdock and Craigmaddie Reservoirs, known as Glasgow's Water Works, were built in the middle of the 19th century as holding reservoirs for Glasgow's water supply, which was piped from Loch Katrine. Queen Victoria turned the wheel that first opened the valve to send this water through the pipes to Milngavie on 14 October 1859.

INFORMATION

Distance: 14.5 km (9 miles), circular route.

Map: OS Landranger, sheet 64.

Start and finish: Milngavie Railway Station car park.

Terrain: Hilly with short stretches of steep gradients.

Refreshments: Mugdock visitors' centre.

Ruins of Craigend Castle.

South Lodge Car Park at the entrance to Mugdock Country Park is an ideal start to the route for those wishing to miss out the fairly steep gradients encountered within the first 1.5 km or so, which, incidently, is the hilliest part of this route. I would point out though, the car park has only space for a small number of cars.

Mugdock Country Park was opened in 1982 and was one of the first of its kind to be opened in Central Scotland. It contains many interesting features and places such as Mugdock Castle, which dates back to the 13th century, built by Sir David de Grahame. It belonged to the famous Graham family who have featured so prominently in Scottish history, with only short interruptions, until this century.

Other places of interest are Moothill, possibly the site of an ancient crannog and a medieval Hill of Judgement; Gallowhill, which until 1718 was the local place of execution; and Craigend Castle. Craigend Castle was designed by James Smith of Jordanhill in 1818 for the Smith family, Lairds of Craigend, who had purchased the land from the Grahams in 1670. The last laird died in 1851 and the estate was passed to Sir Andrew Buchanan, ambassador to the Viennese Court. In this century it was occupied by Sir Harold Yarrow, the Clyde shipbuilder, and George Outram, one of the previous owners of the *Glasgow Herald* newspaper (now *The Herald*). The house and land were sold to the Wilson family in 1946, who owned a zoo in Glasgow, and in 1949 Craigend Zoo opened to the public. It was not a success however, for it closed 6 years later.

Evening reflections on Mugdock loch.

A short distance after entering the park a T-junction is reached. Turn right here and after a further few metres turn right again over a small bridge and continue along this road past Mugdock Loch, the home of many varieties of water fowl, at the other side of which stands the ruin of Mugdock Castle.

Continue along this road to another T-junction where the route continues to the right along an avenue lined by willow and birch to the remnants of Craigend Castle. Just a few metres before this castle is reached, take the road to the left which winds across moorland to the Kyber car park. Stop here and look to the west, where you will see, on a fine day, a breathtaking view over Glasgow and the Clyde Valley.

Leave Mugdock Country Park at the exit at Kyber Pass car park and turn right on to the minor road. After a short downhill stretch the cyclist will have to

A cyclist on Dougalston Road.

commence climbing again but thankfully not for long, for after a few hundred metres the top of the hill is reached. After about 1.5 km or so there is a road junction. Pass this and continue on to a second junction a short distance further on which passes through Mugdock Village, after which it soon joins the A81. Turn right on to this busy road for about 300 m and then turn left on to the minor road at the next junction. Almost immediately, turn right again on to the road which is signed for Balmore. Carry along this road for 1.5 km to another junction and here turn right down a hill and after 200 m turn right again. Follow this road down passed Dougalston Golf Club to the controlled junction with A81 and carry straight on and in just over 100 m Milngavie Railway Station is located on the left.

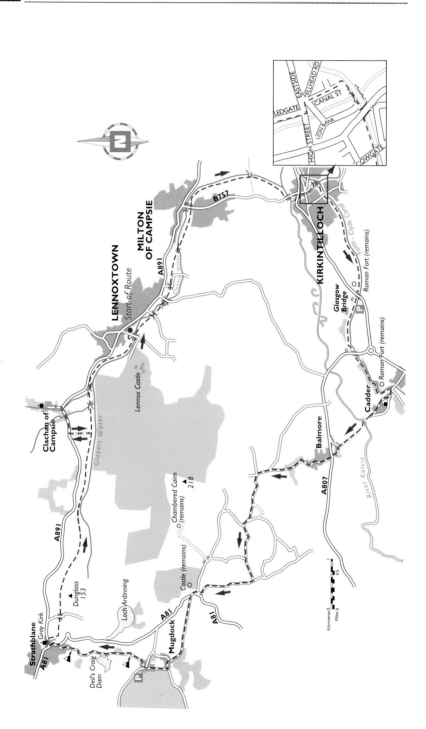

LENNOXTOWN TO STRATHBLANE

The village of Lennoxtown, previously known as Newton of Campsie, was once noted for calico printing and hand-loom weaving, but nowadays these industries have completely vanished. The village is now mainly a residential area for Kirkintilloch and Glasgow. Lennoxtown is also a place where the cyclist can gain access to the Campsie Hills.

This route starts at the car park at the junction of Station Road and Main Street, Lennoxtown. Follow Station Road first down a slight incline to where a bridge crosses over the cycle track, which uses the solum of the former Kirkintilloch to Gartness railway. As the name of the road suggests, this was the site of Lennoxtown Railway Station. Just before crossing this bridge, turn right down a steep and rough set of steps which goes from road level to the cycle track. At the bottom of these steps turn left and commence cycling along this sheltered tree-lined track towards Kirkintilloch. After some 3 km the route passes Milton of Campsie, another village with much the same history as Lennoxtown, although in the 18th century its claim to fame was as a centre for whisky smuggling. From Milton of Campsie it is about 1.5 km along a pleasant wooded path to Kirkintilloch, where the footpath joins the Kilsyth Road. The cyclist should cross Kilsyth Road and then continue by way of the path adjacent to Ledgate, across Eastside and into Canal Street, at the top of which there is a ramp up to the Forth and Clyde Canal, where the route continues westward.

Kirkintilloch originated as Caerpentulach, meaning the fort on the ridge. This fort would have been part of the Antonine Wall. From the 12th century this area was in the hands of the Comyn family, who had their castle at Kirkintilloch. The mote is still visible at Peel Park. Kirkintilloch is an ancient town which was granted Burgal Status by William Comyn, in 1211.

INFORMATION

Distance: 32.2 km (20 miles), circular route.

Map: OS Landranger, sheet 64.

Start and finish: Station Road car park, Lennoxtown.

Terrain: Mainly flat for 20.9 km (13.0 miles) then generally undulating. The short off-road stretch can be muddy in wet weather.

Refreshments: Various places in Kirkintilloch. The Stables Restaurant and Bar, Glasgow Road Bridge, just west of Kirkintilloch. The Coach House, Balmore. Tower Road Aldessan Art Gallery coffee shop, Clachan of Campsie. Kirkhouse Inn, Strathblane.

The Barony was transferred to the Flemings by Robert the Bruce after the Battle of Bannockburn (1314).

Kirkintilloch remained a small predominantly agricultural and weaving community, until the advent of the Forth and Clyde Canal. It would be true to say

A picturesque view of the canal flowing from the centre of Kirkintilloch.

that the town we know today owes much of its development to the canal. In 1773, while work had stopped on the canal further west, Kirkintilloch was operating as Scotland's first inland port, providing access from the River Forth to the east. In 1860 the first shipbuilding and repair yard was opened, and shipbuilding went on in Kirkintilloch until the Second World War. There were also iron foundries because of the relatively cheap transportation of pig iron along this waterway.

Sadly the canal is still culverted under Townhead in Kirkintilloch, but as part of the Millennium Project, both the Forth and Clyde and Union Canals will be re-opened to shipping along their entire length. A new bridge may also be built here.

After crossing Townhead, continue along the canal tow path to Glasgow Bridge, where refreshments can be had at the Stables Restaurant and Bar. This fine Georgian building was converted to its present use in 1981, but as its name suggests it was once the stables where the horses needed for towing the barges were stabled. At the time of its restoration, boats also returned to the canal. A restaurant barge and some pleasure boats operate from here, and in the summer sail between Maryhill and Kirkintilloch.

Another 1.5 km or so further on is Cadder Church, which was the poaching ground of bodysnatchers who supplied the medical profession of the 19th century with bodies for experiments in anatomy. Because of its close proximity to the canal, Cadder Church was an ideal spot for bodysnatching, the canal being a fast and convenient way to transport the bodies to both Edinburgh and Glasgow as the need required. Indeed, this happened so often that the people of Cadder had a watch house built and used iron mort – safes to protect their dead from attack. These can still be seen in the church yard today.

At Cadder Church turn right, away from the tow path, and take the road by the side of the church. There is a gate across this road with a sign which states that this is a private road and there is no through road for vehicles. However, this is a right of way and so can be used by pedestrians and cyclists. Follow this road for 400 m or so at which point a junction is reached. Here follow the path, signposted for Balmore, between the 17th and 18th holes of the Kier Golf Course, which is one of the two courses of the Cawder Golf Club.

After quietly passing through the golf course, cross the River Kelvin by the footbridge. Continue along this narrow path for a short distance to where it turns at right angles, after which it broadens out once again for the remaining 400 m to Balmore. Some where along this stretch of road the path of the Antonine Wall is crossed, but, alas, there is no trace of it left in this vicinity. At the end of this path turn left and follow the road around, passing the lower part of Balmore village, to the junction of the A807. Here cross this road, carefully, and continue through the upper part of Balmore village and on to the junction with Tower Road. Turn left along Tower Road and continue for about 2.5 km to a T-junction. Here turn right and follow this road to the junction with the A81 and then turn right and ride along this busy road for about 300 m to the junction with the minor road to Mugdock. Continue along this road to the village of Mugdock.

Just after the village a T-junction is reached. Turn right here and follow this road for 300 m only, to yet another junction and here take the minor road signposted to Strathblane. This road, which is called Old Mugdock Road, passes Deils Craig Dam before descending the steep hill into Strathblane. On reaching the main road at the junction of the A81 (Glasgow, to Aberfoyle Road) and the A891 (Strathblane to Lennoxtown Road) turn right onto the A891 and travel in the direction of Lennoxtown for 30 m or so. Here on the right a path begins, which is signposted, connecting, once again, to the cycleway on the solum of the disused Gartness to Kirkintilloch railway line.

Just before commencing down this path, stop awhile at the old grey kirk, for here the memories of many historical happenings haunt these hallowed grounds.

The old Church bell at Clachan of Campsie.

The present church dates from 1803, being built on the same site as a much earlier kirk, within which Mary Countess of Angus, daughter of Robert III and sister of James I, lies buried. There is an ancient weather-beaten stone within the church yard which is thought to be a Roman waymarker and which is similar to some others in various locations around the area.

Once on the cycleway continue along it for 8 km to get back to the point where the route began at Lennoxtown. After about 6.4 km a junction with another path is reached, which is signposted to Clachan of Campsie. It is worth the 800 m detour to visit this place, for it is now a craft village with a collection of craft workshops which are open to the public. These include stained glass, jewellery, batiks, children's clothes, painting and picture framing, guitar and violin making and the Aldessan Art Gallery with its fine coffee shop. Last but certainly not least, for the cyclist, there is also a bike shop.

The 9th-century saint, Saint Machan, who was said to be one of the first native-born Evangelists, built the first place of worship in the area of Clachan of Campsie. In 1175 a church was built on the site of his grave. After the Reformation another church was built in its place. Finally when the High Church was built in the 19th century the old church was allowed to fall into disrepair and only a gable is left standing. During the village's face lift in 1993 the old kirk bell, with the date 1729 inscribed upon it, was put on display in the village square. In the graveyard there is the old Mausoleum of the Lennox family dating back many centuries. Other interesting people are also buried

Bicycles parked at Clachan of Campsie.

there, such as John Bell, the Court Physician to the Russian King Peter the Great and William Boick, Covenanter and martyr.

Once back on to the cycleway, a little further towards Lennoxtown, you pass Lennox Castle, which was the seat of the Lennox family until 1927, when it was sold and developed as a psychiatric hospital.

Just as 'the cycleway' reaches the village you will come to the second bridge over the path (the first being at Lennox Castle). Climb to the road above, turn left and follow the road back to the car park.

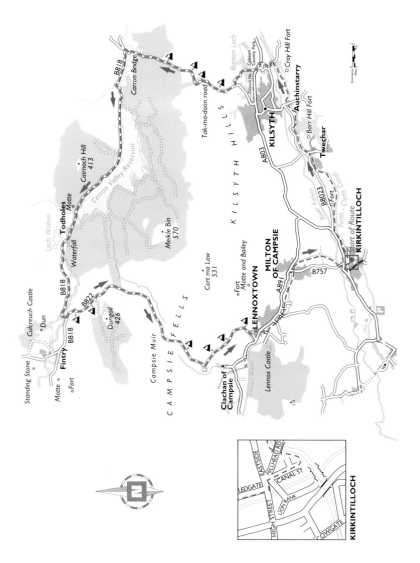

KIRKINTILLOCH

KIRKINTILLOCH TO THE CAMPSIE HILLS

The route begins at the car park at Townhead in Kirkintilloch, adjacent to the tow path of the Forth and Clyde Canal, which forms the first 9.7 km of this route. The Forth and Clyde Canal follows roughly the same route as the Antonine Wall; the reason for this being simply that it is the shortest distance between the east and west coasts of Scotland.

Before the Forth and Clyde Canal was built, ships wishing to get from the west coast to the east would have had to sail round the top of Scotland: a distance in excess of 482.8 km and a very arduous and dangerous journey especially in rough weather. The proposed line of the canal on the other hand was only 56.3 km long. Digging began at Grangemouth on the River Forth in 1768 and took 22 years to complete, finishing at Bowling on the River Clyde in 1790, where the company chairman poured a hogg's head of Forth water into the Clyde. Commence along the tow path of the canal in an easterly direction.

The canal goes on by way of Twechar, a small mining and quarrying village, and passes close to Barr Hill and Croy Hill, which have a Roman fort on each. This area possesses the best stretches of the Antonine Wall to be seen within a short distance from the canal. These Roman remains are easily accessible. Leave the tow path and cross over the canal at the bridge which carries the road into the village of Twechar. Keep to the left side of the road for about 100 m then you will see a track going off to the left. Take this for 400 m up a long hill until a covered circular concrete reservoir is reached, then take the path to the left, through a gate and on another 50 m to Barr Hill Fort. From here there is a very good view of the canal and the surrounding countryside below.

After returning to the tow path at Twechar, continue east, and very soon Auchinstarry is reached. The canal

INFORMATION

Distance: 48.3 km (30 miles), circular route.

Map: OS Landranger, sheet 64 and 57.

Start and finish: Townhead car park, Kirkintilloch.

Terrain: This route is a long distance with some very long steep hills, and is not recommended for children. The worst is the Tak-ma-doon Road, which ascends 263 m in 4.8 km (3.0 miles) with short stretches of up to 1 in 7 gradients. However, the stretch along the Forth and Clyde Canal is flat and this part of the route can be tackled by everyone. Indeed, this 9.7 km (6.0 miles) out/9.7 km (6.0 miles) back route could be used in its own right.

Refreshments: Various places in Kirkintilloch, Kilsyth, Lennoxtown and Fintry. The Carron Bridge Hotel, Carron Bridge.

passes under the B802 (the Kilsyth to Cumbernauld Road) at Auchinstarry, and is spanned by a non-opening bascule bridge. Some 300 m away in the direction of Kilsyth is a disused quarry which has been turned into a leisure area by Kilsyth and Cumbernauld District Council. The floor of the quarry is under water, forming a small loch surrounded by landscaped areas in the foreground with the backdrop of the 30.5 m high whinstone face exposed behind. This is also worth a visit, and, as there is picnic area, it is an ideal spot for a welcome break.

A television crew making a film about the Forth/Clyde canal at Craigmalloch.

On for about another 2.5 km to Craigmalloch, where the canal crosses the road to Dullatur. This is where the main source of water enters the canal, the inlet being right beside the road and running in a lade from Banton Loch 1.5 km away to the north. The loch is reached from the canal and the route continues, firstly by turning north for about 800 m, to the A803, the Kilsyth to Falkirk Road.

On reaching the A803 turn left and follow this road for about 400 m, taking care here for it can be busy, then turn right into Colzium Country Park, the entrance of which is signposted. On entering the park carry on along the road for another 400 m to Colzium House. Banton Loch can be reached by turning right on to a track just before the park car park is reached.

The Battle of Kilsyth (1645), which was part of the Civil War, was fought in the area where Banton Loch now exists. It was a resounding victory for the Marquis of Montrose with his army of

The beautiful walled gardens at Colzium park.

Highlanders, who fought on the side of Charles I against the Covenanter Government of the time. Here we find such names as Slaughter Howe, Bullet Knowe and Drum Burn, testifying to the ferocity of this battle.

Colzium House, formerly the 19th-century seat of the Edmonstones of Duntreath, is now a museum. On past the Clock Theatre, once the stables, to join the Tak-ma-doon Road 200 m further on. Once on the Tak-ma-doon Road the ascent into the Kilsyth Hills begins.

Stop at the top of this long hill to see the spectacular view over nearly the whole of the Forth and Clyde valley. Anyway, after the exertion of the climb a break at this time will be most welcome. It is also worth pointing out that for those who want to do the cycle run along the road at the top of the Campsie Fells, therefore missing out the rigours of the Tak-ma-doon Road, this is where to begin: for the view point has space for about 20 cars. From here it is possible to cycle some 16 km to Fintry and back without encountering any major hills, although the route is not entirely flat.

From here on, the area through which this route passes is one of peace and tranquillity. It is almost like closing

The view west over loch Carron.

a door and leaving the world outside. It is difficult to imagine, while surrounded by such a vast area of unspoilt beauty, that it is only 24 km from the heart of Glasgow and even less to Stirling.

Go along this unclassified road for 3.2 km, through the eastern extremity of Carron Valley Forest, to Carron Bridge, which was built in 1695 to replace a ford that had existed for many hundreds of years as part of the old drove road from Kilsyth to Stirling. This bridge looks larger than it needs to be, with its two span stone arches. This is because the River Carron was much larger before Loch Carron was dammed to make a reservoir.

From here turn left on to the B818. At this point you will encounter the Carron Bridge Hotel, where sustenance can be had.

Around 2.5 km along the B818 is the eastern entrance to the Carron Valley Forest, where an alternative route along forestry roads, skirting the south side of the reservoir, can be found. This route is very picturesque and well worth doing, although it adds a further 3.2 km and some more hills to the journey. However, the 6.4 km route along the B818 is also very attractive with a better surface for cycling.

The routes once again converge at Todholes on the western side of the reservoir and continue on another 5.6 km to the junction with the B822, passing first the Loup of Fintry, where the Endrick cascades over a height of upwards of 30 m from the high moorland into the valley below.

On reaching the B822 it is barely 800 m to the beginning of Fintry, a beautiful and sleepy little village with an ancient past. Back to the route. From where the B818 joins the B822 the road ascends another 150 m in the next 5.6 km, which is of course a mere bagatelle for those cyclists who have recently climbed the Tak-ma-doon Road, although it's still another major hill. But thankfully it's the last, for once at the top of this hill the road begins a steady descent down to Lennoxtown.

Before the final 3.2 km descent down Crow Road to Lennoxtown, stop at the car park, where on a fine day there are wonderful views south over the Kelvin Valley to Glasgow itself and west to Loch Lomond and the Arrochar Alps beyond.

Take care going down the long straight incline on Crow Road: for high speeds can easily be achieved and there is a sharp corner to be negotiated at the bottom. At the end of Crow Road is the junction of the A891. Here cross, taking care, into Station Road. This is where the route from Lennoxtown to Strathblane (see Route 2) began. Continue, as Route 2, down Station Road and turn left on to the cycleway for the last, *flat*, 8 km back into Kirkintilloch.

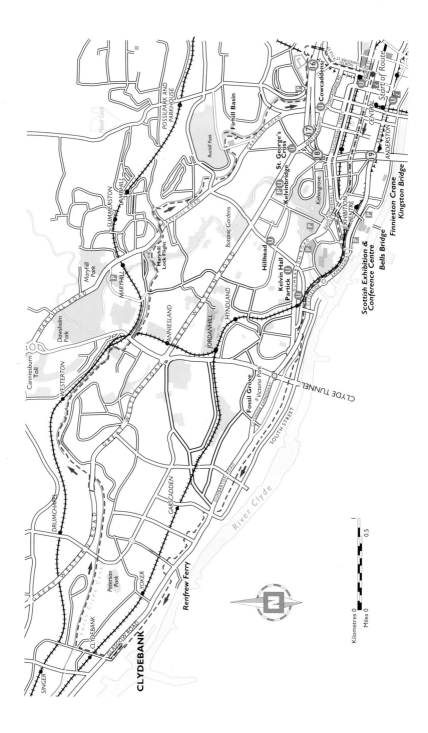

GLASGOW CITY CENTRE TO CLYDEBANK

The route starts at George Square, which is dominated by the City Chambers, designed and built between 1883 and 1889 by William Young to represent, both outside and inside, the grandeur and opulence of this fine Victorian city.

Commence cycling along St Vincent Street carrying straight on past where it merges with Argyll Street. After 2.4 km turn left into Kelvinhaugh Street, at the end of which the Glasgow to Loch Lomond Cycleway commences alongside the Clydeside Expressway. This route is a clearly signposted designated cycleway; therefore, it is not necessary to describe the route but merely to point out the places of interest as they are passed. Opened in 1989 the Glasgow to Loch Lomond Cycleway was the first long-distance cycleway in the west of Scotland, and its 33.8 km has proved popular as a safe off-road route for cyclists and pedestrians ever since. The cycleway officially starts from Bell's Bridge, a few hundred metres to the east opposite Strathclyde Exhibition and Conference Centre, which is also the junction of two other major long-distance cycle routes:

INFORMATION

Distance: 24.1 km (15 miles), circular route.

Map: OS Landranger, sheet 64.

Start and finish: George Square, Glasgow.

Terrain: Generally flat.

Refreshments: Various places in Glasgow. Playdrome cafeteria, Clydebank. Lock 27, Forth and Clyde Canal, north of Anniesland Cross.

A pond surrounded by a riot of colour in Victoria park.

the Glasgow to Irvine, Ardrossan and Greenock cycleway opened fully in 1993 and the Glasgow to Edinburgh cycle route. The latter, which is currently being constructed at various locations along its planned route, is also the route of the Clyde Walkway to Strathclyde Park.

The route runs west parallel to the River Clyde, travelling for some way along the former Lanarkshire Dumbartonshire railway line from Partick through Whiteinch, Scotstoun and Yoker to Clydebank. From there it follows the tow path of the Forth and Clyde Canal through Dalmuir and Old Kilpatrick to Bowling. The final stretch from Bowling to Dumbarton is an off-road path avoiding the busy A82(T) road. After passing through Dumbarton town centre, the route follows the banks of the River Leven to its source in Loch Lomond at Balloch. As far as this route is concerned, it only uses the Glasgow to Loch Lomond Cycleway as far as Clydebank.

On reaching the cycleway, at the end of Kelvinhaugh Street, the Finnieston Crane can be seen clearly a short distance to the east, for it stands 53.4 m above the River Clyde. This imposing city landmark was built in 1932, and had a lifting capacity of 162.5 tonnes. Latterly it was used only intermittently until it was decommissioned in 1994 and turned into an industrial monument. In its heyday however, it was in constant use lifting boilers and engines into ships just completed in the many shipyards of the upper Clyde. It was also used to lift the giant steam locomotives which were exported from Glasgow for use on railways all over the world.

After commencing along the cycleway for just over 3 km, passing en route the massive, red-brick granaries, which today also lie empty, there is a ramp down to Primrose Street in Scotstoun where there is easy access to Victoria Park, one of Glasgow's many beautiful parks. Built partly on the site of an old quarry, Victoria Park is renowned for its formal rock gardens and arboretum. Most famous of all is the Fossil Grove, uncovered in 1887, which is a unique geological example of petrified tree stumps and roots growing some 250 million years ago.

Continuing on the route for 2.4 km, the cycleway passes close to the Renfrew Ferry at Yoker. This river crossing was served for many years by a car ferry between Yoker and Renfrew. The current ferry service, which started in 1984, caters only for pedestrians and cyclists as, since the opening of the Clyde Tunnel, there is no need to transport motor vehicles.

Renfrew ferry.

On entering Clydebank the cycleway leaves the railway line and comes out on to Clyde Street. Here, follow the signs for Loch Lomond. The route carries on through an underpass under Glasgow Road and joins a path which runs parallel to Argyll Road for about 200 m or so, to where it reaches the junction with Barns Street. This is the point where the route leaves the cycleway. Take the street on the opposite side of this road and within a 100 m the tow path of the Forth and Clyde Canal is reached. Here turn right along the tow path heading back in an easterly direction. (On the western side of Argyll Road is the Clydebank Playdrome, where refreshment can be found at its cafeteria.)

Once on the canal the route is once again easy to follow. The canal disappears into a culvert for a short distance at Great Western Road, so from the end of

the canal tow path take the steps up on to the south footpath of Great Western Road. Directly across this road a footpath recommences which follows the line of the canal while it is underground. However, to avoid taking needless risks on this very

The view over Kelvin Grove park with the city of Glasgow behind.

busy road I suggest that it is advisable to walk down to the pedestrian crossing located a 100 m or so to the west, cross the road and walk back to the path on the other side. After a short distance this path joins Blairdardie Road and after crossing this road the canal re-emerges and the tow path begins once again.

Continue along the tow path for a further 4 km, passing en route Lock 27, a hostelry situated right on the canal tow path, where refreshment can be had. Further on now to the Kelvin Aqueduct and Maryhill Lock Flight, to Stockingfield, where the main canal joins the Glasgow branch.

The Kelvin Aqueduct carries the canal 22.9 m above the River Kelvin and is the largest structure on this canal. After the Kelvin Aqueduct has been crossed the tow path climbs through Maryhill Lock Flight. This is the highest part of the canal, the summit level being 47.5 m above sea level.

Until recently the canal was bounded by factories manufacturing rubber products, oil by-products, a dye works, grain mills, and a distillery. In its heyday this part of the canal would have been bustling with barges and other traffic using the Glasgow branch to get to the wharves at Port Dundas. Sadly much of this industry has now disappeared. However this has been beneficial to the canal in other ways, because as the factories have stopped depositing harmful waste it can now support flora and fauna unknown for the last 150 years. You may be surprised by the many varieties of water fowl you encounter on the way along the canal. There are coots, moorhens, ducks and swans, all this before you even come to Ruchill.

Once Stockingfield junction is reached the route continues east along the tow path of the Glasgow branch back towards the city. After 2.4 km, passing along the length of Maryhill, the tow path passes Firhill Stadium, the home of one of Glasgow's several famous football clubs – Partick Thistle.

On the left is Firhill Basin, which was built as a timber basin in 1788. Originally much larger, its purpose was to store logs until they were ready for use by the sawmills. After this point it can be seen that the canal is set quite high, affording a good view over the city centre.

From here it is about 1.6 km to Port Dundas, where the canal ends. As its name suggests, it was built as a port, taking its name from the first governor of the Canal Company, Sir Thomas Dundas. It was built at One Hundred Acre Hill, situated, at the time, above the city of Glasgow. Wharves, basins, granaries, and warehouses were constructed. From its earliest days the canal was used extensively by passenger boats as the quickest and most comfortable way to get from Glasgow to Edinburgh and vice versa. In 1848 the Canal Company stopped its passenger service. By this time the Edinburgh to Glasgow railway had opened, and everyone wanted to travel by train. Other companies ran passenger services until 1876. Pleasure steamers were introduced in 1893 and only stopped at the beginning of the Second World War.

From where the canal ends the route continues right down Craighall Road almost to where it goes under the M8. Here there is a footpath which enters Sighthill Park and within a short distance along this footpath Kyle Street footbridge is located. Here cross this footpath into Kyle Street, turn right into Baird Street and then straight on at the traffic lights into North Hanover Street and straight on down past the junction with Cathedral Street back to George Square.

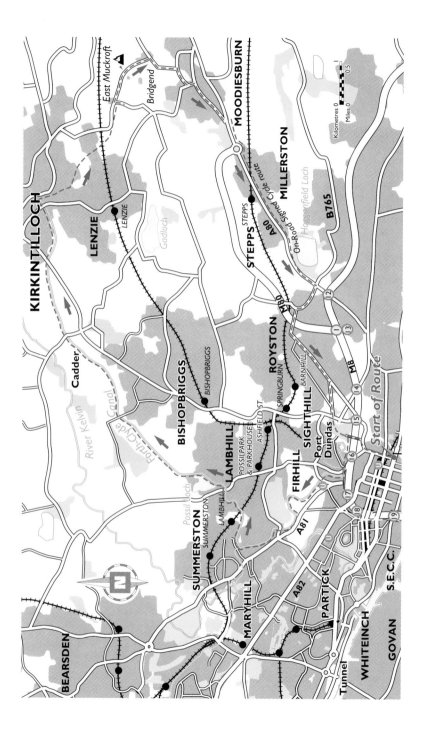

GLASGOW CITY CENTRE TO KIRKINTILLOCH

From George Square to Stockingfield junction on the Forth and Clyde Canal at Maryhill, this route retraces that taken at the end of Route 4. North, up Hanover Street and on to Baird Street then quickly turn left into Kyle Street. Carry on across the footbridge which spans the M8 into Sighthill Park and turn along the path to the left. This path finishes at Craighall Road, at which point carry straight on up this road for 400 m. Take care here for this road is often busy. Join the tow path of the Glasgow branch of the Forth and Clyde Canal at the top of the hill and continue for 3.4 km to the junction of the main canal at Stockingfield.

On reaching Stockingfield junction the route reverts to the eastern tow path of the main canal. To get on to the eastern tow path the traveller must go down the ramp on to Lochburn Road, turn right, under the canal bridge, and staying on the same side of the road go up the ramp to the canal tow path on the other side of the canal.

After 1.5 km or so, the canal passes under Balmore Road Bridge into the district of High Possil, passing close by to Possil Loch, a large area of marsh which is a Scottish Wildlife Trust Reserve with huge stocks of wildfowl wintering and breeding there. Carry on for 3 km to Balmouldie Road, Bishopbriggs, where you will find Bishopbriggs Sports Centre, which contains all sporting amenities including a large swimming pool. Here refreshment can also be had.

Another 1.5 km further on is Cadder Church followed by the Stables at Glasgow Road Bridge (both places are mentioned in Route 2). Only just over 1.5 km further on is Kirkintilloch, where the route leaves the canal tow path.

INFORMATION

Distance: 40 km (25 miles), circular route.

Map: OS Landranger, sheet 64.

Start and finish: George Square, Glasgow.

Terrain: Generally flat but its length might prove daunting to the unfit or inexperienced cyclist.

Refreshments: Various places in Glasgow. Lock 27, Forth and Clyde Canal, north of Anniesland Cross. Bishopbriggs Sports Centre. The Stables Restaurant and Bar, Glasgow Road Bridge, near Kirkintilloch. Various places in Kirkintilloch. Hogganfield Loch (cafeteria in boathouse).

A barge at Bishopbriggs.

The canal is in culvert under Townhead and therefore the tow path comes up to street level at this point. Here turn right and follow the road for a few hundred metres to the road junction, where there is a set of traffic signals. Here carry straight on into Industry Street, where the way is signposted as it enters Woodhead Park. Follow the path through Woodhead Park past Kirkintilloch Baths and then turn right into Parkview Avenue and follow it down to the junction with Lenzie Road. Turn left here and almost immediately on the left is the clearly defined footpath following the line of the Monklands and Kirkintilloch railway. The railway, which was opened in 1826, linked the Monklands coalfield with the Forth and Clyde Canal enabling the coal to be taken by barge to Edinburgh.

Cycle track at Kelvinhall and River Hall.

The 6.4 km to Moodiesburn is no hardship, as for the most part it is very picturesque, following as it does the Bothlin Burn meandering south-east, until the outskirts of Moodiesburn itself is reached. However, a little explanation is necessary in this location. After being on the railway path for 800 m or so a crossing of Garngaber Avenue has to be made. Care should be exercised here, for although this is a fairly narrow road, cars using it tend to be travelling fairly fast. The path continues on the other side of this road, and for the first 100 m or so can be quite muddy. After about another 800 m the path narrows and remains so for about 400 m. Here also the path is immediately adjacent to a post and wire fence and there are steps in two locations within this area. With these slight impediments, which may make cycling difficult, it may be wise to dismount and walk along this short stretch. The route then comes out on to a minor road, where the railway recommences on the other side. However, there are several gates along this next stretch of path which are kept locked at all times, and although there is access for pedestrians, cyclists have to lift their bikes over these gates. There is no reason why cyclists cannot use this path. (The gates are kept closed to prevent farm animals straying.) If this path is used, then in just over 1.5 km it joins Gartferry Road.

Here, however, is an alternative to the use of this path. On joining the minor road turn left and follow it up the short distance to a T-junction. Here turn right and follow this minor road for 800 m to the next road junction. Turn right again and within another 800 m Gartferry Road is reached.

Nesting swans at Maryhill.

At Gartferry Road the route joins the Cumbernauld to Glasgow Safer Signed Cycle Route. Quite a mouthful as was correctly remarked by Strathclyde Regional Councillor Charles Gordon when he officially opened the route as part of National Bike Week in June 1994. This cycle route is the first of a series of routes which has been conceived by Strathclyde Roads as commuter routes at various locations in and around the City of Glasgow. As the name suggests, this route, although on road for much of the distance into Glasgow, should present the cyclist with no problems, for most of it is on designated cycle lanes. Just follow this well-signposted route all the way back to Glasgow.

Turn right on to Gartferry Road and follow the route through Cryston and Muirhead and on to the shared footpath for pedestrians and cyclists along the A80 Cumbernauld Road. On to the segregated on-road cycle lane through Stepps past Hogganfield Loch, where refreshments can be had. Turn right into Provanmill Road then left into Royston Road using a combination of shared footpath and on-road cycle lane. Turn right into Glenconner Park and then right again into Garnock Street and on to Charles Street, at the end of which take the footbridge over Springburn Road and down the cycle path to Pinkston Road. Turn left down the short cycle path, then right into Sighthill Park and left over the M8 by Kyle Street footbridge to where this cycle route officially ends.

At Kyle Street turn right into Baird Street, then straight on at the traffic lights into North Hanover Street and straight on down past the junction with Cathedral Street and into George Square.

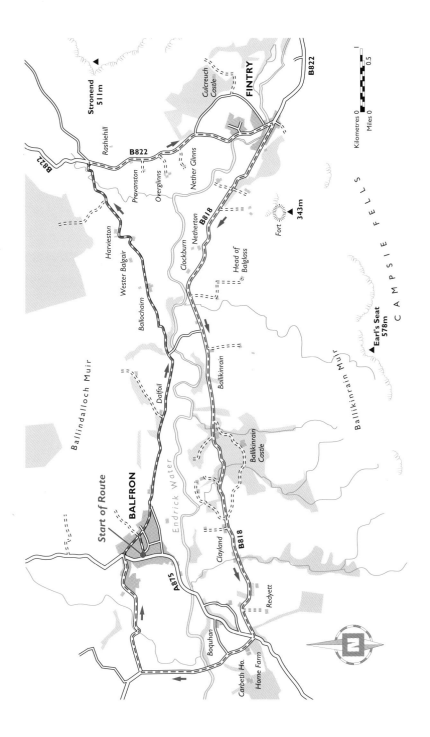

BALFRON TO FINTRY

The attractive village of Balfron tends to be a dormitory village for those people working in Stirling and Glasgow. Its name, according to the Statistical Account, is derived from the Gaelic *Bail-a-bhroin*, which means 'village of mourning'. The reason for this mourning is not known. Throughout the centuries village life was dominated by agriculture, but when Ballindalloch cotton works was built in 1789, the village saw an influx of many people from surrounding areas coming to work there.

In the middle of the 19th century, when the pipeline from Loch Katrine to Glasgow was being laid, the village saw another influx of people to its bounds. This time it was large gangs of predominantly Irish navvies. According to local folklore, one night a serious incident almost took place which, hitherto, has been known as the Battle of Balfron. This was when two large rival factions of navvies, after a bout of serious drinking, faced up to each other with the intention of settling their differences in a violent manner, but before a blow was struck a message was sent to Stirling Castle and a detachment of troops was despatched to break up the mob. If this story is true then all I can say is these opposing armies must have stood looking at each other for a long, long time.

Church corner Balfron.

From the car park head north to the top of the town, past the point where Main Street becomes Buchanan Street and on past the junction with Station Road. Soon after Station Road has been passed, turn right into Spoker's Loan and continue through the junction with Cotton Street into Roman Road. Take Roman Road through the remainder of the village and out

INFORMATION

Distance: 22.5 km (14 miles), circular route.

Map: OS Landranger, sheet 57.

Start and finish: Balfron car park.

Terrain: This route is generally undulating.

Refreshments: Various places in Balfron and Fintry.

into the countryside, where it follows close to the bank of the Endrick Water, gurgling and tumbling, from its source in the Fintry Hills, en route towards Loch Lomond. From this road the view to the south over the Campsie Fells is breathtaking – from Dumgoyne in the west to Meikle Bin and beyond in the east. The colours of these hills seem to be constantly changing as the sun rises and falls over them. Many of the names of the peaks reflect the presence of the area's leading family, the Grahams, such as Graham's Cairn, Earl's Seat and little Earl.

The Clachan hotel in Fintry.

After some 4 km a road junction is reached. Here carry straight on unless you wish to foreshorten the bike ride substantially (if so turn right). From here over the next 2.4 km the road begins to climb slowly and then plateaus out for the next 1.6 km, to where it reaches the junction with the B822 Kippen Road. Here turn right and carry on for the next 2.4 km into the village of Fintry.

The countryside around Fintry is gently hilly with fine grazing land. The plentiful sheep give the area a calm and peaceful image, contrasting with the rugged backdrop of the surrounding Campsie Fells. Therefore, not surprisingly its name, which is of Gaelic origin, signifies 'fair land'.

Culcreuch Castle situated on the edge of the village was built in the 15th century and was the ancestral home of the clan Galbraith. However, most of the land around

The impressive Culreuch Castle.

this area belonged to the powerful and ancient family of Grahams. In the 17th century it belonged to James Graham, the 1st Marquis of Montrose, who conducted a successful campaign, throughout Scotland, against the Covenanters. The castle, although it did not belong to the Grahams, was taken over by a Covenanter army as it marched south from Dundee, in an attempt to engage Montrose's army and prevent them from reaching England. On 14 August 1645 the Covenanters did meet Montrose, at the Battle of Kilsyth, with terrible consequences for the Covenanters. Later the castle was taken over by the Napier family, then it was sold to Alexander Spiers, who was to develop the cotton industry and establish the village of Fintry much as it is today. Culcreuch Castle is now an hotel with part of its grounds turned into a country park.

At the junction of the B811 turn right and follow the B818 back in a westerly direction. The route along the B818 lasts for 9.7 km until it reaches the junction with A875. At this point carry straight through this junction to the minor road signposted for Balfron Station. After almost 2.4 km another road junction is reached. Here turn right and follow this road the remaining 2.4 km into Balfron, joining Station Road. Turn right into Buchanan Street and then on into Main Street and back to the car park.

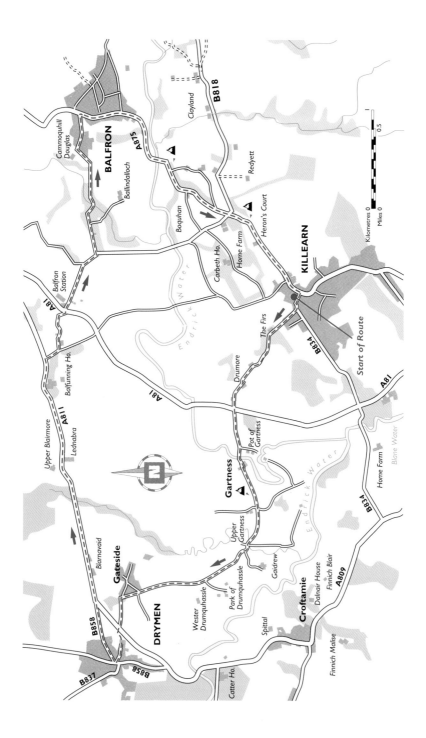

KILLEARN TO BALFRON VIA DRYMEN

This very picturesque route starts at the public car park at the junction of the A875 and Station Road in Killearn.

The village of Killearn lies almost precisely on the Highland Line. It is 91 m above sea level and on a clear day, summer or winter, the views over Loch Lomond and the mountains around it are breathtaking. Therefore, this cycle route as it descends to Drymen then climbs slowly back to Killearn must be one the most beautiful routes to be found anywhere in the surrounding country.

Commence down Station Road, downhill all the way for about 300 m and then turn right into Gartness Road. After 2.4 km this road crosses the A81, which can be very busy so take care. Once on the other side the route soon merges with the West Highland Way, which has by this time joined the road, just before the small village of Gartness and continues all the way to Drymen.

At Gartness, the Endrick Water once again passes under our route, and it is only a short distance from

INFORMATION

Distance: 18.5 km (11.5 miles), circular route.

Map: OS Landranger, sheet 57.

Start and finish: Public car park, Killearn.

Terrain: Generally undulating until the last 3.2 km (2.0 miles) when a series of steeper gradients is experienced.

Refreshments: Various places in Killearn, Drymen and Balfron.

Rapids at Pot of Gartness.

this spot that the Pot of Gartness is located. At this famous beauty spot the Endrick falls over a rock which spans the river into a deep pool at the bottom. Often salmon and sea trout can be seen forcing their way up through the torrent of water to the spawning grounds further on.

John Napier of Merchison, inventor of logarithms, is said to have been born at Gartness in 1550 and lived there at various stages throughout his life, including the time around 1614 when he was perfecting this mathematical system. After crossing the bridge over the Endrick Water, the road starts to climb. This short sharp uphill stretch lasts for about 300 m and is quite steep in some places. This is followed by a short undulating stretch before the road once again starts to wind uphill; this time for about a further 400 m until it reaches the highest point of this road, then finally drops down through Gateside and on to the junction with the A811 Dumbarton to Stirling Road.

To cycle into Drymen from here turn right and follow the A811 for about 400 m to where it merges with the B858. Here double back along this road for a further 400 m into Drymen. However, a quicker way is to dismount, cross over the road and take the pedestrian ramp up, a hundred metres or so, to where it joins the Gartness Road once again, which quickly winds down to the centre of Drymen.

The small, but attractive, village of Drymen is a busy place throughout the year, particularly at weekends and holidays, for it is one of the most popular destinations for Glaswegians and others out on an afternoon drive. The village itself, whose name is of Celtic origin and means ridge or knoll, describing the physical features of the land around the district, is very old, with records of a church being in existence as far back as 1248. Throughout its long history

Attractive cottages Killearn.

the village has been home to those people who worked the lands belonging to the Duke of Montrose, who was the landowner of most of this district.

Once ready to leave Drymen join the B858 in the direction of Stirling for 400 m to where this road merges with the A818 and turn left along it. Carry on for 3.2 km to a minor road on the right which is signposted to Balfron and take this road. After about 150 m turn left, which is still the Balfron Road, and continue to the junction of the A81. Cross over the A81 into the minor road opposite, called Indies Road. This is Balfron Station, which used to be on the, now-disused, Caledonian Railway's Glasgow to Stirling line. Within this small cluster of houses the theme would seem decidedly 19th-century colonial, for as well as Indies Road there is an Indian Cottage and an Indiesdorp – *dorp* being the Afrikaans word for a cluster of houses.

Once past this remnant of the British Raj, continue along this road for a little over 1.6 km to the next junction. Here turn left and follow this road, which becomes Station Road, into Balfron.

A view of the Arrochar Alps from the Killearn road.

At the traffic lights turn right on to the A875 and after going through the village the route continues on this road for a further 3.2 km back to Killearn. This part of the route is uphill all the way with some fairly steep stretches along its length.

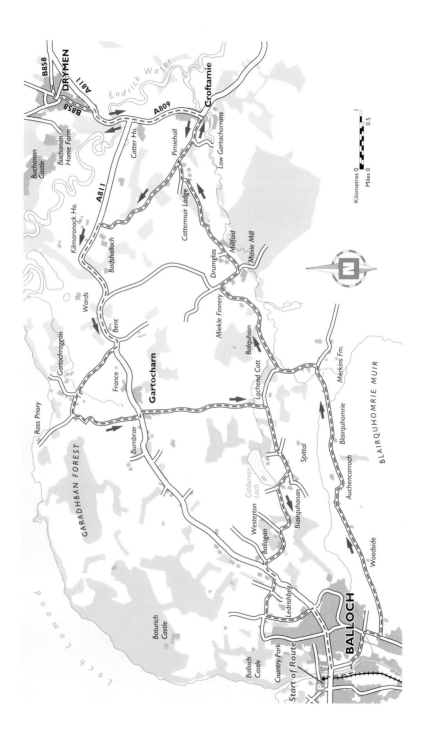

Kilometres 0

Miles 0

0.5

DRYMEN

B858

B858

A811

Buchanan Castle

Buchanan Home Farm

Catter Ho.

Endrick Water

A809

Croftamie

Pirniehall

Low Gartachorrans

Kilmaronock Ho.

A811

Badshalloch

Cattermuir Lodge

Millfaid

Movie Mill

Drumglas

Wards

Bent

Gartochraggan

Miekle Finnery

Balquhain

France

Gartocharn

Lochend Cott

Merkins Frm.

Ross Priory

Burnbrae

BLAIRQUHOMRIE MUIR

Blairquhomrie

GARADHBAN FOREST

Caldarvan Loch

Spittal

Auchencarroch

Westerton

Blairquhanan

Ballagan

Woodside

Baturich Castle

Ledrishbeg

Balloch Castle

Country Park

Start of Route

P

BALLOCH

Loch Lomond

BALLOCH TO DRYMEN

The community at Balloch has developed in modern times through tourism. The first pleasure steamer service on Loch Lomond, the *Marion*, was started in 1818 and there have been pleasure steamers plying up and down the loch ever since. The railway arrived here in 1850, which increased the area's appeal particularly to day trippers from Glasgow.

This route starts in Balloch at the car park opposite the Railway Station. From here follow the cycle route signposted in the direction of Dumbarton along the west bank of the River Leven. After 800 m turn left across a bridge over the river and after a short distance turn right on to the A813. Carry along this road for 800 m and turn left into Auchencarroch Road. The road climbs fairly consistently for the next 3.2 km through Blairquhomrie Muir with its heather clad and mossy slopes. As there are no particularly steep inclines to contend with along this stretch and as the prevailing wind is at the cyclist's back, no real problems should be encountered here. Once at the top of this hill the route stays relatively flat until the descent into Balloch almost at the end of the journey. This road is a pleasant, minor, country road with little traffic to bother about. However care must be taken, for at various points along the way some double bends have to be negotiated.

INFORMATION

Distance: 28.9 km (18 miles), circular route.

Map: OS Landranger, sheets 56, 63 and 64.

Start and finish: Car park opposite Balloch Railway Station.

Terrain: Generally undulating.

Refreshments: Various places in Balloch, Gartocharn, Croftamie and Drymen.

Boats on the river Leven at Balloch.

After being on this road for about 5 km a 4-way junction is reached. Here turn left, following the sign for Croftamie, and travel past Caldarvan Station, which reminds us that there was once a railway in these parts. After 800 m a T-junction is reached. Still following the signs for Croftamie, turn right. This very pleasant road continues for another 1.6 km to where once more a T-junction is reached. Follow the sign for Croftamie, so turn right along this road past Mavie Mill and on to the junction at Pirniehall. Here turn right and follow the road to Croftamie. At Croftamie join the A809 through the village, taking great care at the junction of the A811 a little over 1.6 km further on. Once on the A811 the route passes over the beautiful 5-spanned stone bridge crossing the Endrick Water. It is then but a short distance to the B858, which is the road into Drymen.

Loch Lomond.

At this point in the journey, the cyclist has the opportunity, if so desired, of continuing onward using the cycle route to Killin, which from the village of Drymen continues northward using the extensive forestry tracks through the Garadhban Forest and the Queen Elizabeth Forest, passing, en route, Aberfoyle and Callander. The Killin cycle route is intended to link into the Glasgow to Loch Lomond cycle route. It is also to become part of the Sustrans, Inverness to Dover route, parts of which are already in place – notably, the Glasgow to Irvine cycle route.

For the purposes of this route, however, after Drymen has been explored or refreshment has been partaken of, return to the junction at Pirniehall by the same route in reverse. From this junction, this time take the right fork on to the minor road signposted for Gartocharn. This road falls steadily to the junction of the A811, and at this point turn left along this road. Although this A-class road can, of course, be busy, it should not cause concern for cyclists. However, it will do no harm to take care when cycling here. The route uses this road for about 3 km before turning right at the junction signposting a campsite. This is a loop road, which, although slightly longer in length, takes the cyclist to Gartocharn by a more peaceful and picturesque route. However, the road surface is quite bumpy in places. This road passes close to Ross Priory, which was owned by the Buchanan family, once so powerful in these parts. It has now been taken over by the University of Strathclyde as a sports and social club. On the second half of this loop, as the road rises slightly towards Gartocharn, there are splendid views of the loch and over the mountains, which so dramatically separate the Highlands from Central Scotland. While gazing over this remarkable sight it is not hard to imagine this terrain being carved out by melting glaciers at the end of the Ice Age.

On reaching the village of Gartocharn turn left along the A811 for about 200 m and turn right into School Road. This road climbs steadily for 800 m, at which point it flattens out. After being on this road for 2.4 km a T-junction is reached. Here turn right and follow the sign for Balloch. After 1.5 km or so this road descends fairly steeply back downhill. Take care not to go too fast down this hill, for there are two very tight double bends to negotiate before the road once again joins the A811. Here turn

Drymen.

left and follow this main road once again for about 800 m and then turn right into Drymen Road and carry on along this road, now in Balloch, for about 800 m back to the car park opposite the railway station.

Well worth a visit, at this point, is Balloch Castle and Country Park, where more magnificent views of the south end of Loch Lomond can be seen. The castle was built in 1808 for John Buchanan of Ardoch. The estate was bought by Glasgow Corporation in 1915. The grounds were turned into a public park, which it remained until 1981, when it became a Country Park, with the castle becoming its visitors' centre.

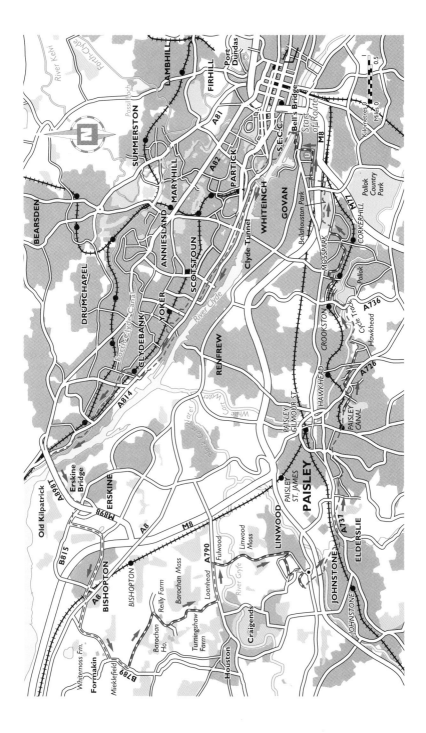

BELL'S BRIDGE: GLASGOW TO ERSKINE BRIDGE

This route utilises two of the main long distance cycle routes in the area: the Glasgow to Loch Lomond cycle route and the Glasgow to Irvine cycle route. The Glasgow to Loch Lomond cycle route has already been described as far as Clydebank (see Route 5). This is a well-signposted cycle track and there should be no difficulty in negotiating the route.

At Clydebank first cross Argyll Road at the Toucan Crossing, which is a specially designed crossing for pedestrians and cyclists, and continue along the tow path of the Forth and Clyde Canal.

Clydebank is the birthplace of the 3 Queens of the Cunard Line. These great ships, the *Queen Mary*, *Queen Elizabeth* and *Queen Elizabeth II*, were built at the famous John Brown's shipyard in the centre of Clydebank. Clydebank itself was built in the latter part of the 19th century around the shipyards which were springing up on that part of the Clyde. Because of the large concentration of heavy industry, Clydebank suffered very badly during the Second World War. Between the 13 and 14 March 1941 German bombers dropped hundreds of tons of bombs on the town, killing 534 people and injuring 790 more, with 4,300 houses destroyed, and another 7,700 badly damaged. In all only 8 houses in the town were left standing intact.

The canal crosses Dumbarton Road at Dalmuir and continues on following close to the River Clyde. After about 3 km the tow path comes to Old Kilpatrick, where the Erskine Bridge spans the River Clyde.

Old Kilpatrick gets its name from a Celtic word *Kill* meaning church or cell and Patrick being called after Saint Patrick, so meaning the church of St Patrick. It is said by some historians that he was born in this area. Others say he was born further east in New Kilpatrick

INFORMATION

Distance: 50 km (31 miles), circular route.

Map: OS Landranger, sheet 64.

Start and finish: Scottish Exhibition and Conference Centre car park, Glasgow.

Terrain: Generally fairly flat but its distance might be daunting for the unfit or inexperienced cyclist.

Refreshments: Various places en route.

beside the loch of St Germains, which is now in Bearsden. As a boy, while fishing off a tidal rock at Old Kilpatrick, Patrick was captured by pirates and taken off to Ireland, where later he was canonised and ultimately became the country's patron saint.

At Old Kilpatrick just before the canal commences under this gigantic road bridge leave the tow path, cross the canal bridge and turn left on to the A814. Carry on along this road, under Erskine Bridge, for almost 800 m to a junction on the right which is signposted for Glasgow. Go along Station Road and commence uphill past Kilpatrick Railway Station and continue almost to the bridge under the A82. Here turn left into Mountpleasant Drive, which winds round to a bridge. At the other side of this bridge is a signpost pointing out the cycle route across the Erskine Bridge.

Cycle track and the river Clyde from the Erskine Bridge.

The way across this 2.4 km-long cable-stayed box-girder bridge, the deck of which is 55 m above the river, can be an exhilarating experience. However, I can assure the reader it is quite safe. Stop for a while at the centre of the main span for a look at the view back over the entire distance you have covered on this route thus far.

On the south side of the bridge the cycle path winds down to join a roundabout. On the west side of this roundabout it joins the B815 and the continuation of the route. I recommend that here it would be better to dismount and walk to the B815, therefore avoiding this busy roundabout. Here is also the entrance to Erskine Hospital, which looks after so well the men and women who have lost limbs while in service with the armed forces.

After joining the B815 carry on for just over 800 m to where Erskine Parish Church is located. Opposite this beautiful old building there is Drumcross Road, which heads south. Take this road for 1.2 km to the junction with Old Greenock Road. Here turn right and follow this road all the way through the village of Bishopton. Follow signs for Greenock through the village. The route joins the A8 only to leave it again immediately, by turning left on to the minor road, which is, in fact, still Old Greenock Road and which is signposted for Houston and Johnstone. After about 1.5 km a three-way junction is reached. Here turn left following the signs for Formakin. This road winds downhill towards the Formakin Estate, and as you ride down you will notice a high perimeter fence on the left, inside which is the Royal Ordnance factory, where high explosives are manufactured. On this road one can see for miles over the length and breadth of Renfrewshire.

At the bottom of the hill is Formakin Estate, which was built between 1902 and 1913 for the rich Paisley stockbroker John Augustus Holms.

A short distance after passing Formakin the route joins the B789. Turn left here, for 800 m or so to the junction with Reilly Road. Turn left into Reilly Road, which is a very quiet 3 m-wide unclassified road. The first section of this road runs adjacent to the southern boundary fence of the Royal Ordnance factory but

Gryffe Water.

then the road turns into open country, on past Turningshaw Farm to the junction of the B790. Here turn left along this road for 800 m to the road signposted for Linwood on the right. Turn here and carry on over the bridge spanning the Gryffe Water and after 2.4 km the route enters the town of Linwood.

On entering Linwood turn right into Brediland Road (which is the road before the give-way sign). Then take the first on the right, which is Erskinfauld Road. Travel to the end of this road and turn left into Clippens Road, being mindful here of the traffic, for this is a bus route. The route only uses this busy road for a few hundred metres before turning right into Cowal Drive, which is the street before the roundabout. At this point there is a signpost for the cycleway.

Carry on to the end of Cowal Drive and turn right into Muirhead Drive, and at the end of this road the cycle track commences. Turn left on to the cycle track and follow this into Elderslie, the birthplace of Sir William Wallace (1274–1305), and then on to Paisley.

Paisley is an ancient place which was founded about 560 by a missionary Irish monk called Mirin, who set about building a small church on the east bank of the Cart. (Hence the name of the local football team.)

In 1163 Walter Fitzalan founded Paisley Abbey with 13 monks whom he had brought from a Cistercian order in Shropshire, his own native land. The abbey was damaged by fire; first by Edward I, whose army set it alight in 1307, and then again in 1498. However, undaunted, the monks always had it rebuilt. The monastery

Paisley Abbey.

was closed in 1560 during the Reformation, when Paisley Abbey then became a Protestant church. Paisley Abbey is a church of great beauty well worth a visit.

From the 18th century Paisley became famous for two industries: the weaving industry and the thread industry. In the middle of the last century the Coats family was famous for manufacturing a cotton thread strong enough to be used in the new revolutionary Singers' Sewing Machine from America, soon to be manufactured on the other side of the Clyde at Clydebank.

Paisley has many fine Victorian buildings, which include the Town Hall and the Observatory, gifted by the Coats family to the town in 1882, and has been recording astronomical and meteorological information ever since. Continue along the cycle route to Glasgow, where the route ends at the south side of Bell's Bridge.

There is a set of extremely informative, easy-to-use, leaflets for both the Glasgow to Loch Lomond cycle route and the Clyde Coast cycle routes (of which Glasgow to Paisley and Paisley to Greenock are part). This series of leaflets is available at all tourist information centres.

It is not necessary to describe the route in detail, for it is adequately signposted, but, instead, I shall describe the places of interest that you will pass.

At Crookston Road it is worth taking a small detour of a few hundred metres to where Crookston Castle can be found. This 15th-century stone fortress, which was the residence of Sir John Stewart of Darnley, whose descendant Henry Stewart (Lord Darnley) married Mary Queen of Scots in 1565, stands on top of a defensive mound constructed in the 12th century by Sir Robert Croc. Croc, who was a feudal tenant of the Royal House of Stewart, built a settlement next to this defensive mound. Crookston derived its name, from Croc's toun, *toun* meaning 'settlement'. At Mosspark Boulevard the route enters Bellahouston Park, one of the city's 70 public parks. In 1938 the Empire Exhibition was held here, the centre piece of which was a 91.4 m high tower, which was itself built on top of Bellahouston Hill some 52 m above sea level. It also had the biggest amusement park in Europe. Even though it rained almost every day, 13,500,000 people visited the Empire Exhibition within its duration. Another part of this exhibition was the Palace of Art, which still stands today. Bell's Bridge, at the end of the route, is a fully operational swing bridge allowing shipping access further up the river as far as the weir 800 m beyond. These days this is normally confined to the *Waverley*, the last Clyde paddle steamer, and the occasional high-masted yacht.

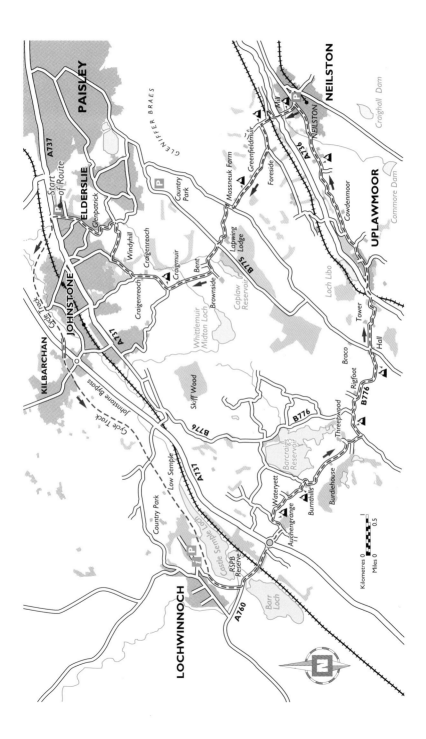

ELDERSLIE TO LOCHWINNOCH VIA UPLAWMOOR

Elderslie (previously known as Ellersly), which was once a village on its own, now forms part of the Paisley/Johnstone conurbation. It is, however, a very historic place with evidence of a settlement going back to the Bronze Age about 2,300 years ago.

The best-known family to have lived in the area were the Wallaces of Ellersly. Their castle would have been situated where the Wallace monument stands today. The first member of the Wallace family to settle in Scotland was Richard de Wals, a Norman Knight who came north with King David I in 1124 and settled in Ayrshire. It was his son, Sir Malcolm Wallace, who built the castle at Elderslie. He married Margaret Craufurd, the daughter of the Sheriff of Ayr, and there in 1270 his son William was born. William Wallace was the great hero who did so much for Scotland in the War of Independence, until his horrific death at the hands of the English in 1305. He was caught and taken to London, where at a mock trial he was sentenced to death, then barbarously executed by being hung, drawn and quartered and his head nailed to London Bridge.

In more modern times Elderslie has been famous for its carpets: for here was the location of Stoddard's carpet factory, which was world famous for the production of high-quality carpets for almost a century.

The route starts at the car park in Stoddart Square opposite the Public Library. Turn right out of the car park and then turn right again into Glenpatrick Road. Immediately ahead is the controlled junction at Main Street. Cross this into Canal Street, at the bottom of which the Glasgow to Irvine/Ardrossan cycleway continues along the disused railway towards Johnstone. However, in just over 800 m the way comes to the Johnstone bypass, where a footbridge

INFORMATION

Distance: 24.1 km (15 miles), circular route.

Map: OS Landranger, sheets 63 and 64.

Start and finish: Stoddart Square, car park, Elderslie.

Terrain: The first part of this route is generally fairly flat, but after Lochwinnoch there are areas of fairly steep hills some quite prolonged, particularly so between Neilston and Elderslie. If however one does not wish to over exert oneself then turn at Lochwinnoch and return again via the cycle route.

Refreshments: Various places in Elderslie, Lochwinnoch and Uplawmoor.

now spans this new road. This is the junction of two cycle tracks: the one crossing the footbridge is to Greenock via Kilmacolm and the other continuing along the east side of the bypass goes by way of Johnstone to Irvine and Seamill.

Johnstone has been marked on maps for many hundred years. The Old Brig at Johnstone was the only place to cross the Black Cart Water all the way to the River Clyde some miles to the north, so Johnstone would have been on the road through Renfrewshire from Paisley to Ardrossan. Johnstone or Ihonstoun, which just means 'John's settlement', was designed and built as a town in 1782 to house the families of the miners and quarriers who worked in the pits and quarries around the area. Also in this area there was a tradition of linen thread spinning. Physically joined to Johnstone to the south-west is Kilbarchan, which the route bisects. The latter was an 18th-century weaving village with its 2-storey cottages, which were both home and weaving shop. One of these cottages has now been taken over by the National Trust for Scotland and completely restored to its former glory, representing how it would have looked in the 18th

Cyclists rest at Castle Semple visitors centre.

century. Its loom is still in working order, and weaving demonstrations are given at certain times.

For the next 6.4 km along this well-defined cycleway, the route is through pleasant wooded countryside until it reaches Lochwinnoch, the latter 3.2 km being along the banks of Castle Semple Loch.

Lochwinnoch, meaning 'Saint Winnoc's loch', is where the traveller gains access to the first Regional Park created in the country. This fine park opens a 36.3 sq. km area of countryside to the public all the way from Lochwinnoch to Cloch Point on the Clyde coast with nature trails, bird sanctuaries, moorland, rivers, lochs and woodland. Most of this land is privately owned, with the owners allowing people the right to roam. So be vigilant: keep to the prescribed paths; keep control of your dogs; and don't start fires. Castle Semple water park is also part of the regional park area offering facilities for all sorts of water sports. The third area of interest is the Royal Society for the

Cyclist on a tree lined part of the route.

Protection of Birds' Nature Centre, with an observation tower, nature trails and bird-watching hides. These facilities are all well signposted from Lochwinnoch, which is itself an attractive rural village, with a small agricultural museum. It's worth noting though that the entrance to Muirshiel Park is some 6 km from Lochwinnoch, leaving by way of the B786 Bridge of Weir Road and then on to the unclassified road to Muirshiel.

At Lochwinnoch the route leaves the cycleway at Church Street by carrying straight on at the point where the cycle route turns right. Carry on along Church Street over the River Calder and turn left on to the A760, which can be quite busy so take care. Follow this road, past the Nature Centre almost opposite Lochwinnoch Railway Station, for 1.5 km to the roundabout, which forms the junction with the A737. Here continue straight on, once around the roundabout, to the unclassified road which is signed

Auchengrange Hill leading to Belltrees Road. This road commences uphill fairly steeply, for 400 m to the junction with Belltrees Road. Here turn left and continue along this road after first stopping to survey the view of the valley below. On a further 400 m to where another junction is reached and where a right turn should be made. This quiet minor road continues uphill at various gradients, some of which are fairly steep, followed by a short but steep descent down to yet another junction, which is adjacent to the wall of Barcraigs Reservoir, where a right turn is made. Uphill again past Newmills Cottage, after which the gradients increase for a short distance. On the way up this hill there is a good view over the Barcraigs Reservoir. This is a very picturesque part of the route with many fine views over Kirkleegreen and Cuffhill Reservoirs on to Cuff Hill and Lochlands Hill. Thereafter the road commences downhill, turning left at the next 2 junctions encountered. On now for 800 m to the junction with the B776, where a right turn is made towards Uplawmoor. Once again commence uphill for 800 m and then descend down to the junction with the B775, at which point a fine old baronial hall can be seen on the right. Straight on through this junction to where this road meets the A736. Here turn left and join this busy road for 200 m or so before turning right into the village of Uplawmoor. Carry on through this picturesque village and join the road signposted for Neilston 4 km ahead. At Neilston Main Street turn left into Holehouse Brae and carry on downhill, past Coats's mill, alas now not in use, to the A736 once again. Here turn left and immediately right on to the minor road which carries on over the Lochliboside Hills to Johnstone. This is when the road really starts to climb steeply, and it does so for about 1.5 km, passing en route a T-junction, at which the road to the left should be taken. At the top of this hill pause for a look at the view over towards Paisley and on as far as Glasgow. Here turn right at the white house and follow the road along to Mossneuk Farm. Here turn right. Then after only 200 m turn left and continue to the B775. Cross this T-junction and continue along this minor road, which descends for most of the way, for 4 km, following signs for Johnstone. Take care on this stretch for there are two double bends to negotiate.

On entering the upperpart of Johnstone this road becomes Auchenlodment Road. Continue along this road for about 1.6 km to the junction with Kings Road, which veers off to the right (just before the fire station). Take Kings Road a short distance then turn right into Cemetery Road. After passing the cemetery this road changes its name to Abbey Road. Continue for 400 m to a T-junction and turn left into Glenpatrick Road. Carry on almost to the end of this road, at which point turn right into Stodart Square, where the route began.

Farmyard scene.

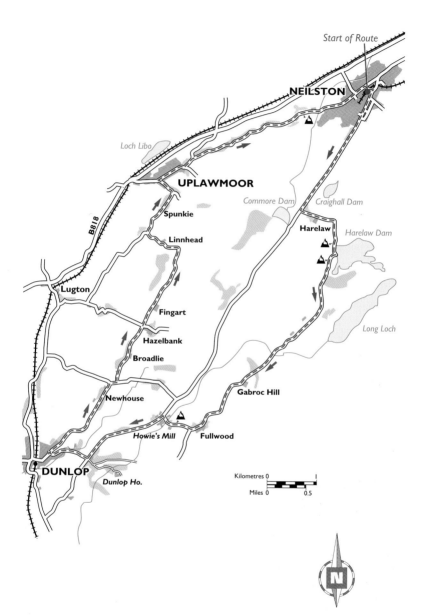

Start of Route

NEILSTON

Loch Libo

UPLAWMOOR

Commore Dam   *Craighall Dam*

Spunkie

Linnhead

Harelaw   *Harelaw Dam*

B818

Lugton

Fingart

Long Loch

Hazelbank

Broadlie

Newhouse

Gabroc Hill

Howie's Mill   **Fullwood**

DUNLOP

Dunlop Ho.

Kilometres 0 _____ 1
Miles 0 _____ 0.5

N

NEILSTON TO DUNLOP

Neilston was merely a small collection of houses until the Industrial Revolution, although there is evidence of a church existing in the area since the 12th century. The village grew rapidly owing to the availability of fresh clean water, being an ideal spot to set up industries such as thread mills, calico printing, dying, bleaching and laundries. However, by the middle of the 19th century all but the thread mill had ceased to exist. Today Neilston has become a dormatory town for Paisley and Glasgow and has increased greatly in size. This is due in part to the reopening of the railway in the 1970s.

At Neilston Station car park turn right into Corseton Brae and carry on along this road as it winds uphill, sometimes quite steeply, for 3.2 km. At this point turn left, at a crossroads, along the unclassified road towards Harelaw Dam. Just before the road reaches the dam there is a short but very steep gradient to contend with and just as the road begins to flatten out another even

INFORMATION

Distance: 24.1 km (15 miles), circular route.

Map: OS Landranger, sheet 64.

Start and finish: Neilston Railway Station car park.

Terrain: This route is generally undulating with 2 short stretches of very steep hills gradient about 1 in 5.

Refreshments: Various places in Neilston, Dunlop and Uplawmoor.

Harelaw dam.

steeper section has to be negotiated. However, soon the top is reached, where fine views over Harelaw Dam, the adjacent Long Loch and the surrounding countryside can be had.

After about 1.5 km the road leaves Renfrewshire and enters north Ayrshire, where it continues for an undulating 3.2 km to a junction. Here on a clear day there are wonderful views over to the Isle of Arran with a white cap of snow on top of Goat Fell. Turn right down a hill for 800 m, past Howie's Mill to the junction just beyond. Here turn left and follow this road towards Dunlop turning right at the next road junction, which is opposite Dunlop House.

Hedgerow in bloom.

The route continues on another 800 m to a junction. Here turn right and follow this minor road as it gradually climbs uphill for about 1.5 km, at which point it levels out for a short distance before reaching a T-junction. Here turn right and follow the road signposted for Uplawmoor, which within a few metres turns left at the next road junction. Follow this fairly flat road straight on through the next junction for

4 km to a T-junction, at which point turn right. On the west side of the road, on a farm called Spunkie, there is most handsome herd of Highland cattle. As the road enters the village of Uplawmoor, it becomes Tannoch Road and this joins Neilston Road opposite Caldwell Parish Church.

Uplawmoor was first mentioned in a Charter of James, Chancellor of Scotland, in 1294 as the Uplayis, meaning, in this case, a place lying outside Paisley Abbey lands. However, this sleepy little village changed little until this century, relying, up until then, on hand-loom weaving and agriculture for its population of 200 to make its living. Today this attractive village, which lies almost on the border with Ayrshire, is mainly a residential area for those working in Glasgow or Paisley.

Turn right on to Neilston Road and continue through the village. On the way through, the route passes Uplawmoor Inn, which was said to have been a hideout for smugglers from Ayrshire. This of course was a long time ago, for today it is a pleasant hotel with a beer garden at the rear facing out on to the village green. From this vantage point one can keep an eye on the bikes while partaking of some refreshment and watching the village cricket team play.

Cyclist in the streets of Dunlop.

At the end of the village veer left onto the road which is signposted for Neilston. The last 4 km into Neilston is mainly flat until the village is reached and then the road climbs up to join Main Street. Just before the centre of the town turn right into Station Road and back to the station car park.

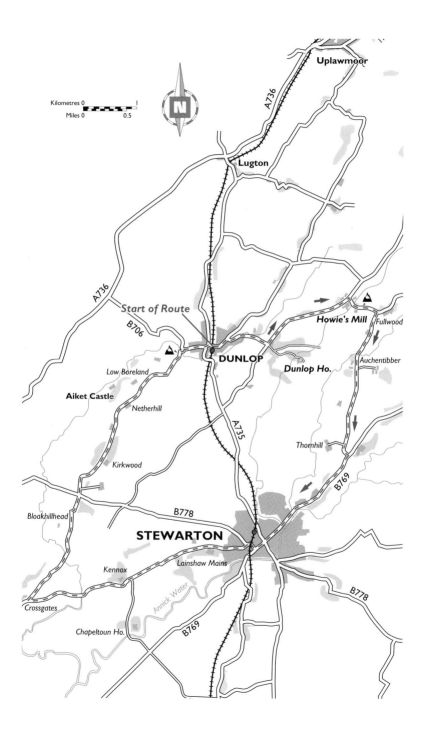

Uplawmoor

A736

Kilometres 0 | 1
Miles 0 | 0.5

N

Lugton

A736

B706

Start of Route

Howie's Mill Fullwood

DUNLOP

Dunlop Ho.

Auchentibber

Low Boreland

Aiket Castle

Netherhill

A735

Thornhill

Kirkwood

B769

Bloakhillhead

B778

STEWARTON

Kennox

Lainshaw Mains

Crossgates

Annick Water

Chapeltoun Ho.

B769

B778

DUNLOP TO STEWARTON

The village of Dunlop is built on the site of a fort, which would have been constructed by one of the many noble Norman families who were granted lands in this area by King David I in the 12th century. This mainly agricultural village is famous for a type of cheese which takes its name from the village. Barbara Gilmore, the wife of a local farmer, had to take refuge in Ireland because she was a Covenanter. There she learned of a different process of cheese making which, on her return home, she developed into the well-known Dunlop cheese.

Dunlop, which has now been declared a conservation area, is a very interesting and picturesque village with its rows of traditional 18th-century terraced cottages, the Parish church built in 1835 and Kirkland House built in 1781, which was once the manse.

INFORMATION

Distance: 20.5 km (12.7 miles), circular route.

Map: OS Landranger, sheet 63 and 64.

Start and finish: Dunlop Railway Station car park.

Terrain: Generally flat with undulating stretches.

Refreshments: Various places in Dunlop and Stewarton.

Kirkland house, Dunlop.

This route begins at Dunlop Station car park. Turn right out of the car park on to Newmill Road. Soon a road junction is reached, at which point turn right following the larger of the two roads. After about 800 m turn left on to a minor road opposite the entrance to Dunlop House and carry on for 1.5 km to Howie's Mill. Here turn right down by the side of the mill and follow this minor road, as it climbs, to the next junction. Turn right here and carry on, downhill, to the junction with the B769. Follow this road for 2.4 km into Stewarton.

Whitewashed cottages in Dunlop.

Carry straight on through Main Street in Stewarton to the mini roundabout and take the B778, signposted for Kilwinning. After a short distance this road passes under a railway bridge and a little further on another junction is reached. Here take the left fork on to the minor road (called Stewarton Road) leaving the B778 at this point. After 1.6 km the road starts to wind uphill for about 400 m and then it levels out for a bit before climbing again for another 400 m. Turn right 4.8 km from Stewarton and follow this road, also a minor road, back to the junction of the B778 a further 2.4 km. At this junction carry straight on over this road and continue along the minor road on the other side back in the direction of Dunlop. This road winds uphill quite steeply for a short distance and then continues to climb much more gradually for about 800 m before levelling off. The road then carries on along the top of an escarpment, which provides an excellent view of the valley below. In this valley is situated Aitket Castle, which was built by Alexander Cunningham in 1479. The original 4-storey tower was added to and altered over the centuries, but sadly it was badly damaged by fire in 1957. Since then the castle has undergone a major restoration programme by its present owner. However, it is not open to the public.

View over Stewarton.

The road then commences downhill into the village of Dunlop. After crossing the bridge which spans the Glazert Burn, the road climbs up to the junction at Main Street. Turn right here and follow the road up to the centre of the village. Then turn left on to Stewarton Road, quickly right into Newmill Road, over the railway bridge and back to where the route began at Dunlop Station.

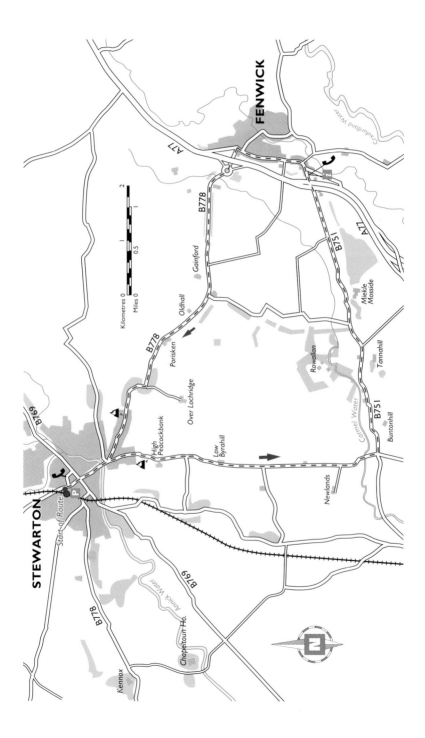

STEWARTON TO FENWICK

At Stewarton Railway Station car park turn right on to Rigg Street. Take care here for this is a busy road, and follow it down and through the junction with Main Street into Vennel Street.

This town takes its name from the first High Steward of Scotland, Walter Fitzalan, who was appointed by King David I and who was granted lands in the area. His descendant, also called Walter, married Robert the Bruce's daughter Marjory. When their son Robert succeeded to the throne in 1377, he was the first of the Stewart dynasty to rule Scotland for the next 3 centuries. Stewarton is, however, best known as the Bonnet Toun and has existed as such since 1650, or at least that is when records of the trade were started, but it is likely that bonnets were made in this area long before that time.

On reaching Vennel Street, continue uphill to a junction and carry straight on the Kilmaurs to

INFORMATION

Distance: 14.5 km (9 miles), circular route.

Map: OS Landranger, sheets 64 and 70.

Start and finish: Stewarton Railway Station car park.

Terrain: Generally undulating.

Refreshments: Various places in Stewarton and Fenwick.

Fenwick Parish Church.

Kilmarnock Road. Carry along this minor road as it winds uphill for 1.6 km, to where a fine view of the Firth of Clyde as far south as the Ailsa Craig can be seen. This undulating but very straight road continues to the junction of the B751 road to Fenwick, after 4.8 km.

Turn left and after about 1.5 km the road passes Rowallan Castle, which is situated by the Carmel Water a little to the north. This imposing castle, a mix of architecture from the 13th, 15th and 16th centuries, was the birthplace of Robert II's wife, Elizabeth Mure. It has, fairly recently, undergone extensive renovation and is not open to the general public. Continue on for 3.2 km to where this B-class road joins the A77. Extreme care must be taken at this very busy junction. I would recommend that those trying to negotiate this road should dismount and walk across. On the other side the B751 continues into Fenwick.

At the top of the town take the B778, which is signposted for Stewarton, slowly climbing for about 3 km along this quiet road to the highest point, where once again, on a clear day, incredible views over the Firth of Clyde and south Ayrshire can be seen. The road then starts its quite steep descent into Stewarton, so take care. After entering the town, the road joins the minor road to Kilmaurs. Turn right at this junction and retrace the route through Vennel Street, on to Rigg Street and back to Stewarton Station.

Opposite:One of the many covenanters graves in Fenwick Parish Churchyard.

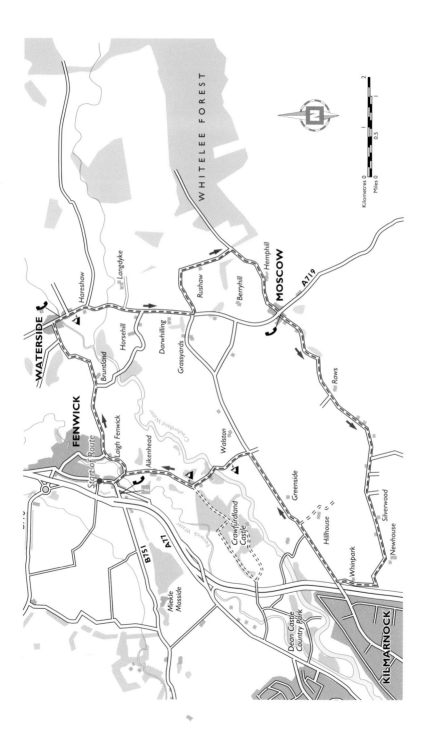

FENWICK TO MOSCOW

Fenwick today is mainly a residential village but in the 18th century hand-loom weaving was established in Laigh Fenwick, which is the lower part of the town.

There are no public car parks in Fenwick, therefore the route starts from Main Street, which is the B751, where there are no parking restrictions. Turn into Waterside Road, which is signposted on the west side of the B751, and after only about 200 m turn left, still following the signs for Waterside. The first 2.4 km of this route are uphill with the latter part being quite steep, which is almost the whole way to Waterside. At this very small but picturesque village, situated beside Crawfurdland Water, turn right on to the A719, which is the Galston Road, and continue down this undulating road for 2 km. At this point a 4-way junction is to be found. Turn left here and follow this very narrow minor road to the entrance of Raithmuir Farm and turn right. The road surface here is a little bumpy. Carry on to a T-junction, turn right and follow the road downhill to Moscow.

INFORMATION

Distance: 17.7 km (11 miles), circular route.

Map: OS Landranger, sheet 70.

Start and finish: Main Street, Fenwick.

Terrain: Generally undulating, with short stretches of steep gradients.

Refreshments: Various places in Fenwick.

Cyclists making their way up Waterslap, Fenwick.

Sadly the folklore that has associated this little village with its larger namesake in Russia cannot be in anyway substantiated. Its name is thought to have been derived from the word Mosshaugh, meaning a corner of peaty moorland, and why it should have been changed to Moscow can only be a matter for conjecture. One explanation is that, in the 19th century, the name was probably changed as a gimmick because of news being reported about the Napoleonic Wars and has stuck ever since. To enhance the Russian flavour of the area the local burn was named the Volga. Furthermore the village was visited by the Soviet Prime Minister Alexei Nikolayevich Kosygin during his visit to Scotland in 1965.

The mystery surrounding this little village is not confined to its name, for it is also the scene of one Scotland's most notorious unsolved murders. On 12 March 1884 Mr Robert Rankin, a respected business gentleman of Kilmarnock, was found brutally murdered by strangulation in his home in Volga Bank Cottage, Hemphill, Moscow. Mr Rankin had also received many blows to the head and other parts of his body. Strangely the assailant had tried to make this brutal attack look like suicide by placing a hammer into the dead man's hand. Although how the murderer could have expected the police to accept that the victim had struck himself about the head, face and body with a hammer many times and with such ferocity that he brought about his own death is difficult to understand. Although a man was detained the following week on suspicion, no evidence could be found to implicate him and he was subsequently released. To this day this crime has remained a complete mystery. The murder caused such a stir in the area that a local Kilmarnock newspaper reported

The bridge over Crawfurdland water.

that 'on Sunday last, Moscow was visited by large numbers of visitors from the town [Kilmarnock], attracted thither by morbid curiosity and the fineness of the weather. The village Inn was literally besieged by thirsty travellers, who were admitted in relays until the entire stock of liquor was exhausted'. The reason for this interest was simply that, at this time, there was no serious crime in the parish of Kilmarnock and the act of murder was completely unheard of.

Another point of interest in Moscow is a house (also in Hemphill) which has a stained-glass front door in the design of a Soviet Russian postage stamp depicting the crest of the Federation of Soviet Farmers. This house is currently owned by Mr and Mrs Matt Donald, who don't mind people stopping to have a look at their interesting door.

The present owner beside the once 'notorious cottage', Volga Bank Cottage, Moscow.

The route continues over the A719 following the minor road which is, for the next stretch, still undulating. At 10.5 km there is a junction but the route is straight on following the sign for Kilmarnock. At this point, on a clear day, there is a beautiful view over the Firth of Clyde as far as the Ailsa Craig, and in particular the Isle of Arran shows itself to its splendid best. After another 2.4 km this road begins to run parallel to the A77 for a short distance but then soon comes to a T-junction. Here turn right, at the sign for Waterside, and follow this road uphill once again, for another 2.4 km to the junction with the Fenwick Road. Here turn left into this road and soon it goes over a beautiful stone bridge which spans Crawfurdland Water. At this point this fast-flowing stream has gouged a 91 m deep gorge out of the surrounding landscape. This is close to Crawfurdland Castle (not open to the public), the ancient home of the Crawfurd family, which dates from the 14th century, and which still belongs to the family today.

This road now continues on, through pleasant gently rolling agricultural land, for the remaining 2.4 km back to Fenwick.

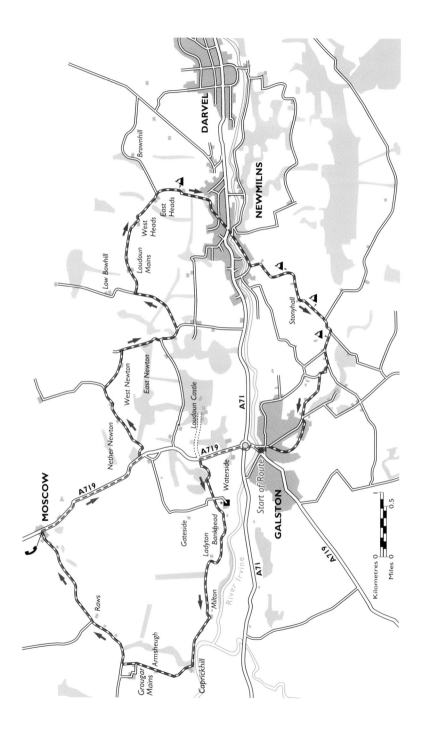

GALSTON TO NEWMILNS
VIA MOSCOW

Galston is located 6.4 km east of Kilmarnock. Due to the town lying within a fertile valley on the River Irvine, there has been a settlement in Galston for many thousands of years. There was a Roman camp here which served the garrison situated on top of Loudoun Hill, a few miles to the east.

Some of the places of interest include Barr Castle, which was built in the 15th century and where John Knox preached in 1556, and St Sophia's Church, which is unusually built in the Byzantine style. Perhaps this church's architectural style, and it being given the name of an East European saint, adds some credence to the myth of this area's association with Russia!

The route starts at Wallace Street. Start off in a northerly direction and carry on over the bridge which spans the River Irvine and within a short distance a major roundabout is reached at the junction of the A71 and A719. I recommend that you dismount here and negotiate this very busy roundabout on foot; along the adjacent footpaths and at the other side recommence cycling along the much quieter A719. After only 800 m on this A-class road, turn left on to a very quiet minor road, which is in fact the first junction located after passing the roundabout.

Head downhill, following this road past a beautiful little pond, which is the home to many varieties of wild fowl. After a short distance the road begins to run alongside the River Irvine. It then begins to wind uphill away from the river to a road junction at about 5 km out. Here carry straight on up the hill for a further 800 m to a T-junction and turn right following this undulating road into Moscow, 3.2 km further on. In Moscow when the crossroads with the A719 is reached turn right on to this road. Although this is an A-class road, it is seldom very busy. However, care should be taken nevertheless, for there will certainly

INFORMATION

Distance: 24.1 km (15 miles), circular route.

Map: OS Landranger, sheet 70.

Start and finish: Car park off Wallace Street, Galston.

Terrain: This route is very hilly and not recommened for the inexperienced or unfit cyclist.

Refreshments: Various places in Galston and Newmilns.

View through the portals of Loudoun Castle.

be fast-moving traffic using it. After only 2.4 km, however, it's goodbye to this road. Here turn left on to a minor road marked by a blue sign with B&B and Whatriggs on it. This road winds up a shallow hill for a little over 800 m to a junction, at which point carry straight on. This road can be considered one of the best cycling roads in the area. Follow it down into a beautiful wooded valley and over a narrow bridge. Just south of here lies the ruins of Loudoun Castle, tragically burned down in 1941. It was first built as a tower house in the 16th century and then lavishly turned into a grand mansion in the 18th century and was the home of the Campbells, the Earls of Loudoun. In 1647 John Campbell the 1st Earl, together with the Earl of Lanark and the Earl of Lauderdale, visited Charles I while the King was imprisoned in Carisbrooke Castle in the Isle of Wight. There they signed the 'Engagement' whereby the Scottish Lords promised the King military assistance in return for his agreement to establish Presbyterianism in England over a period of 3 years. Ironically less than 40 years later a group of Covenanters was imprisoned in the castle. The local men from Newmilns made a successful rescue attempt, setting the castle on fire as they made their escape.

The Loudoun Estate is now a Castle Park with many facilities, such as a museum, woodland walks and nature trails, and much to keep the children occupied. Access to the estate is off the A719, just after the roundabout north of Galston.

At the next junction turn left and commence uphill for a little over 1.6 km past Loudoun Mains. Stop for a while to admire the beautiful views over the Irvine valley below, and also the hills further south, for they are without doubt splendid. After passing East Head Farm another road junction is reached. Turn right and follow the road steeply downhill past the Dry Ski Slope into Newmilns.

Newmilns became a Burgh of barony in 1491. Its old town house, built in 1739 in the traditional Scottish style with bellcote crownsteps and forestairs, is now the information centre. As with Darvel and its westerly neighbour Galston, Newmilns grew with the cotton and coalmining industries.

At the bottom of this hill the A71 is reached. Turn left here and then immediately right again into Brown Street. I suggest once again you dismount and continue on foot.

On entering Brown Street carry along this to its end. Here take the left road which sweeps uphill and over a bridge and then carry on uphill, which is very steep in places, for almost 2.4 km. (To allay your worst fears however the very steep gradients are over short distances – although one is of the order of 1 in 7.)

The Townhouse in Newmilns.

Old mile marker in Newmilns.

Once again there are fine views to be seen at the top of this hill, especially on the other side of the Irvine valley from whence you came.

At the next road junction carry straight on and commence the descent back into Galston. This next section of road has many junctions, which are as follows: first, straight on; second, after a little under 800 m, turn right; third, only a short distance further on, turn left; fourth, now within Galston, turn right into Cessnock Road, which becomes Station Road; fifth, turn right into Wallace Street and hence back to the start of the route.

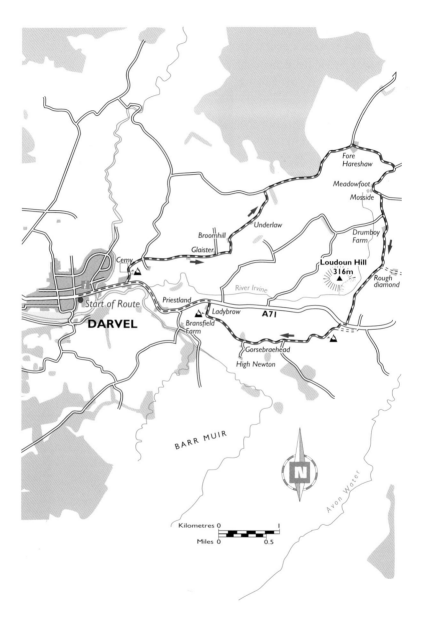

Fore Hareshaw

Meadowfoot

Mosside

Underlaw

Broomhill

Glaister

Drumboy Farm

Cemy

Loudoun Hill
316m

Rough diamond

Priestland

River Irvine

DARVEL

Start of Route

Ladybrow

A71

Bransfield Farm

Gorsebraehead

High Newton

B A R R   M U I R

Avon Water

N

Kilometres 0 ——————— 1

Miles 0 ——————— 0.5

DARVEL AND ITS SURROUNDS

Darvel was a planned town built at the beginning of the 19th century, which grew from the linen industry and then coalmining. The weaving industry was revolutionised in 1876 when Alexander Morton introduced the power loom into the mills of the town and set up the manufacture of lace. Today many of the mills are still in existence, but only for the manufacture of knitwear.

In Hastings Square there is a bust of Alexander Fleming, the famous bacteriologist, who was born on a farm just outside the town. In 1928 he discovered the first antibiotic, penicillin, which was a giant step forward for medical science.

From the car park at East Mains Street turn right and follow this busy trunk road to the outskirts of the town. Just past George Young Drive, the entrance to a housing estate, the small unclassified road veers off to the left. Take this road. It immediately commences uphill steeply, but not for long: for after passing the cemetery less than 400 m away, the road flattens out.

INFORMATION

Distance: 16.1 km (10 miles), circular route.

Map: OS Landranger, sheet 71.

Start and finish: Car park off East Mains Street, Darvel.

Terrain: Generally undulating with short stretches of steeper hills.

Refreshments: Various places in Darvel.

Left: The Town square in Darvel.

Below: Main Street in Darvel with Loudoun hill in the background.

After about 1.5 km carry straight on at a crossroads up a slight incline, which continues gently rising for 2.4 km. At just over the 4 km point there is a road junction; turn right and continue uphill past the southern extremity of Whitelee Forest. After 6.4 km a series of 3 road junctions begins in fairly quick succession: first turn right, then 800 m on turn right again and at the last of this series, a short distance further, carry straight on.

A puncture being fixed at the roadside by a member of the Cyclist Touring Club.

There is now a splendid view of the 316 m-high Loudoun Hill. This is a volcanic plug which was scoured by glacial movement into a crag and tail formation. The Romans built a large garrison on Loudoun Hill, from which vantage point they could control the local Celtic tribes who lived around the area. Under this hill is the site of a minor battle of the War of Independence. It was here, in 1307, that Robert the Bruce defeated the English under the command of the Earl of Pembroke. It is also interesting to note that the other great Scottish hero of the Wars of Independence, William Wallace, was also involved in a skirmish here, against the same foe, some years before.

At just over 8 km, as the road begins its descent back down towards the A71, there is a very tight double bend to negotiate, so care should be taken here.

At the junction with the A71 turn right and follow this main road for about 300 m to where an entrance to a quarry is located. Turn left here and pass the quarry entrance, where just beyond a minor road begins. Take care here for the road surface at this quarry entrance is very rough indeed. Follow this very picturesque and quiet road for almost 3.2 km to where it once again joins the main road. The day I cycled this road I was escorted part of the way by hares, who had no difficulty in winning their race against this sluggish cyclist. Turn left and re-join the main A71 and follow it, downhill, through the small village of Priestland and on to Darvel, 800 m further on.

Wild brambles.

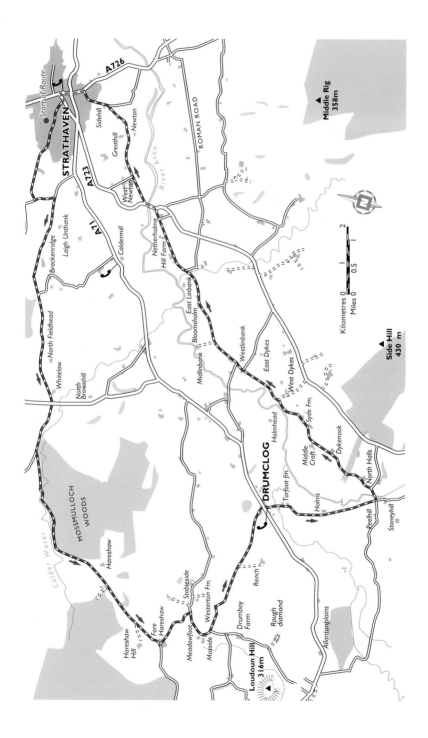

STRATHAVEN TO DRUMCLOG

Strathaven, its name meaning wide valley of the River Avon, is a small picturesque market town which has managed to hold on to its traditional character. The area within the vicinity of Strathaven has supported settlements of people for over 2,500 years and has always been easily accessible by visitors from the south. Some of these visitors were welcome; others were much less so. The Romans were early visitors to the area, and one of their military roads ran from Carstairs through Sandford, just to the south of Strathaven, to Loudoun Hill.

In the town the Boo-Backet Bridge (which means highly arched) is reckoned by some to have been built

INFORMATION

Distance: 24.1 km (15 miles), circular route.

Map: OS Landranger, sheet 71.

Start and finish: Car park off Glasgow Road, Strathaven.

Terrain: Generally mildly undulating.

Refreshments: Various places in Strathaven.

in Roman times. Others tend to think, and I agree with them, that this bridge was built much later, probably in feudal times, on the site of the original Roman Bridge.

Boo Backet Bridge in Strathaven.

Not much seems to be known about the family who became the feudal Lords of Avondell during the time of the reign of David I, but by the early 15th century it was in the hands, possibly through marriage, of the powerful Douglas family. There must have been some form of keep in the area dating from the 14th century, and it's very possible it would have stood on the same site as the castle that can be seen today. This castle was built by Lord Avondell, but it was seldom lived in and was eventually allowed to fall into disrepair. There is a legend associated with the castle. A lord of the castle was so incensed by his wife's infidelity that he had her bricked up within the cavity of a wall, but this 'generous' lord had also included a last meal of bread and water to be put in with her. Later in the 19th century bones were discovered when part of a wall fell down. It is not recorded if a plate and a cup were found next to the remains.

Next door to the castle is the town's mill, which was built by the Duke of Hamilton in 1650 for the local people to have their corn ground. It was used as a mill until 1966, latterly for grinding oat meal. It was taken over by the town's Arts Guild in the 1970s and refurbished as a theatre and arts complex.

There is also a fine museum in Strathaven called the John Hastie Museum. John Hastie, who was a local grocer living at the end of the 19th century, bequeathed the money to build a park and museum for the good of the residents of Strathaven.

The route begins at the car park off Glasgow Road.

Commence west past the boating pond into Threestanes Road, turn left here and follow this road until it joins Lethame Road. Here turn right into Lethame Road, which takes you out of the town and on to an unclassified road. Follow this road for 1.6 km to where a road junction is located. Here turn left and then after only a short distance turn right at the next junction and follow the signs to Darvel.

Cyclist checking the map while using this route as part of his journey from John O'Groats to Lands End.

Close to this road is the site of the Battle of Drumclog, where, in 1679, 250 poorly armed Covenanters defeated a troop of the King's Dragoons led by John Graham of Claverhouse.

After 4 km a crossroads is reached. Carry straight on here to a fork in the road and go left continuing on to the next junction a further 4 km away and turn left. Carry on now to the next junction only a short distance away and this time turn right. On now another short distance to yet another junction and this time carry straight on and after 2.4 km the little village of Drumclog is reached.

Drumclog was too small to have been shown on General Roy's map in the 18th century, so the small collection of buildings that forms this hamlet must be fairly recent. However, at the edge of the village of Torfoot, Roman coins were found in 1806 when drains were being dug. Also to the south of the village at Peel Farm an Iron Age settlement has been excavated. In 1912 Drumclog Memorial Kirk was built in remembrance of the nearby battle.

Within this church is a stained-glass window depicting the Covenanters and a replica of their banner is hung in the Chancel (the original is held in the John Hastie Museum).

Drumclog Parish Church.

Cross the A71 and head down the B745 for 2.4 km to the first crossroads. Here turn left, still on this B-class road, and cross the bridge that spans the Glengaven Water. A few metres further on at the next road junction take the minor road on the left. Carry along this picturesque road, which is one of the most tremendous cycling roads I have come across anywhere, for the next 6.4 km to the junction with the A723. At this point turn left and cross the bridge over the River Avon and turn immediately right and head uphill for 400 m. When this road enters Strathaven it becomes Newton Road. At the end of Newton Road turn left into Todshill Street. Then cross Kirk Street into Main Street, which joins Common Green, at the end of which carry straight on into Lethame Road, where there is an entrance to John Hastie Park. From here, it is only but a few metres to the car park where the route began. (Please remember to dismount and walk within John Hastie Park.)

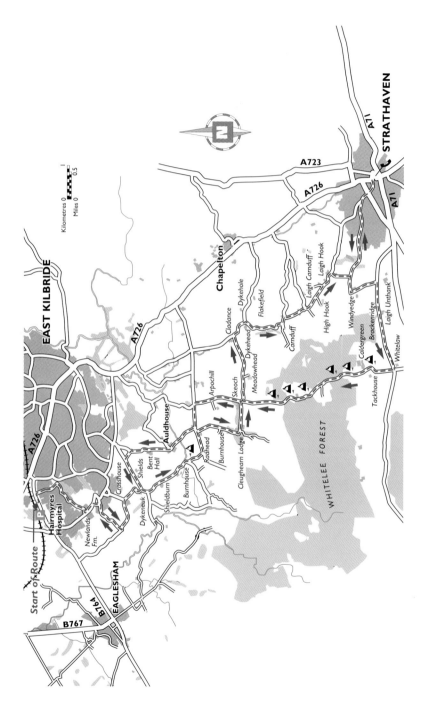

EAST KILBRIDE TO STRATHAVEN

 East Kilbride is Scotland's first post-war 'New Town'. It was started in 1947 and is now the sixth largest town in the country. At its heart however is the charming old village, which still manages to retain its original character. Most of the buildings in the village date from the 17th and 18th centuries but of course there has been a settlement here since before feudal times. During the 17th century the people of this district were staunch believers in the Covenanting cause, and many men from East Kilbride Parish fought at the Battle of Bothwell Brig. The flag they carried into battle, known as 'The Kilbryde Flag', can still be seen in the Kelvingrove Museum and Art Gallery in Glasgow.

One of the many interesting buildings in the village is the Montgomery Arms, which was built in the 17th century as a coaching inn. Outside the front stands the 'Loupin on Stane'. This large rectangular stone with steps up the one side was there to help people, who had perhaps partaken of a drop too much, get back on their horses.

For people living around East Kilbride cycling must be one of the most pleasurable pursuits with the wonderful network of minor roads existing in this area. These roads are very quiet and picturesque and can be used, by all the family, for cycling in relative safety. Indeed they can only be described as a cyclists' paradise. Although I have selected specific routes in this district it will soon be seen that once one has familiarised oneself with this unique network of roads, many different routes can be devised allowing many hours of cycling pleasure in this area. These minor roads are seldom used by motor vehicles, but of course as they are still part of the public road system, cyclists should still remain vigilant and mindful of vehicles which may be travelling along them.

INFORMATION

Distance: 41.8 km (26 miles), circular route.

Map: OS Landranger, sheets 64 and 71.

Start and finish: Hairmyres Railway Station car park off Eaglesham Road, East Kilbride.

Terrain: This route is very hilly, but only within the latter stages. I shall therefore also describe shorter and less hilly alternatives.

Refreshments: Various places in Stathaven.

This route begins at Hairmyres Station car park. Hairmyres is one of the ancient boundaries of Kilbride marked by a celtic cross which can still be seen today in the grounds of Hairmyres Hospital. Turn left and carry along Eaglesham Road, past Hairmyres Hospital, for almost 400 m. Take care here for this can be a busy road. Turn right into Windward Road and then immediately right again into Westport. (Alternatively as Westport is situated parallel to Eaglesham Road, cyclists can access it from the footpath at the eastern end, which directly links Eaglesham Road, and then take the first right into Dunedin Drive.) From here turn left and carry on all the way along Dunedin Drive to the junction with Mossnuek Road and turn right.

Continue along Mossnuek Road to Wellesley Crescent and turn left. Carry on along this crescent to where a formal footpath is located on the left. Take this footpath for a short distance to a junction and turn left and within a few metres turn right and after only a few metres more this footpath joins Eden Grove. Carry on uphill to Eden Drive, at the end of which turn left into Greenhills Road. After passing Newlandsmuir Road cross over Greenhills Road and down a pedestrian ramp on the right into Newlands Road, past Londsdale Farm and turn right. As you cycle down this road you will notice the town ends and the countryside begins. Here begins the series of roads illustrated both in this route and the next.

The auld House Inn.

At the first junction turn left and carry on as the road winds uphill. It was close to here that Lickprivick Castle would have been situated. Alas, however, there is no trace of it left today. This castle belonged to the Lickprivick family, who were appointed Sergeants and Coroners of Kilbride by John Comyn in 1290, and who later conspired, with Comyn, against Robert the Bruce.

After 1.6 km a T-junction is reached and here turn right following signs for Auldhouse. After a few metres take the left fork and on past Burnhouse Farm. After 2.4 km a T-junction is reached which is signed for Auldhouse to the left. Turn right here and then quickly take the left fork up a steep hill for a short distance and after passing Raehead Farm turn right at the next junction. This road continues for 1.6 km to where it turns at right angles when it passes Cleughearn Lodge. Bear left here and continue on to the crossroads, at which carry straight on. This stretch of road has sheep farms on both sides, and at Meadowhead Farm a flock of Jacob's sheep can be seen.

The next junction is at Cladance, where my described route turns right. However, for those wishing an easier route to follow turn left at this road junction and follow this road for 1.6 km to the next junction. Here turn left and follow the signs for Auldhouse. When this hamlet is reached, carry straight on following signs for East Kilbride along this undulating road for almost

Duck pond by the roadside.

1.2 km and then turn left. After 400 m turn left again. After a further 1.2 km turn right on to the road which is signed for Jackton. After 1.6 km a crossroads is reached: here turn right (opposite the road which is signed for North and South Allerton). This is now the road which you left the bounds of East Kilbride at the beginning of the route, so follow the same route, in reverse, back to Hairmyres Station. This route is 16.5 km long and is predominantely flat.

Back to the main route after turning right at the next T-junction less than 800 m further on. Follow this road as it ascends gradually through scenic moorland for over 1.6 km before it starts downhill towards Strathaven. Along this stretch of road, which continues for 4.8 km, there are 3 road junctions: fork right at 2 of them and turn right at the third. Here there are good views over Lanarkshire, with Tinto Hill clearly visible some kilometres to the south.

Carry along this road for 400 m to where a T-junction is reached and turn left. Follow this road downhill into Strathaven, where it becomes Lethame Road. At the end of Lethame Road where it joins Townhead Street carry straight on into Common Green, which is the picturesque centre of this charming town (see Route 17). The outward part of this journey is 19.3 km.

After you have explored the town and perhaps partaken of some refreshment, the way out of Strathaven is back the same way as you entered, that is back up Lethame Road. At the point where you joined the road which became Lethame Road the main route carries straight on. This is also where the second alternative route begins: simply turn right and follow the same route taken in the outward journey to the junction at Cladance. At this point follow the easier route described above, until Hairmyres Railway Station car park is once again reached. This alternative, although it is not any shorter in distance to that of the main route, avoids the steepest gradients encountered on it.

Back once more to the main route. Having gone straight on at the junction, carry on 400 m to the next and turn left. This minor road winds downhill for another 400 m to a T-junction, where a right turn is made in the direction of Darvel. This road ascends very gradually for some 4 km until a crossroads is reached. Here turn right back towards East Kilbride.

This road, which ascends some 90 m over 4 km, starts gently enough, but as it progresses towards the summit and Whitelee Forest the gradients get very steep in some places. I would not recommend this route to families with children or to the less fit, unless you are prepared to walk intermittently along this 3.2 km stretch. Whitelee Forest is a modern commercial pine forest which was planted on the moorland. Many hundreds of years ago it would also have been covered by forest, for it was part of the Caledonian Forest, which covered a large area of Scotland. The area was populated by many small groups of Celtic people, who lived by hunting the wild animals of the forest.

If you are fit enough to cycle or are prepared to dismount and walk, then the view that awaits you at the summit is very worth while indeed.

There is an incredible view over East Kilbride and the other Lanark-shire towns, Glasgow, the Campsie Fells and Ben Lomond, and the Firth of Clyde as far as the Isle of Arran. In fact one can see, at once, over all the areas covered in the 25 routes of this book.

Cyclist nearing the summit at Whitelees forest.

Once over the summit, the road commences the descent towards East Kilbride passing straight across a crossroads en route. Care should be taken on this steep descent for very high speeds can be achieved if one is not very careful. At the end of this road turn left and quickly pass one junction before turning right at the next, following the sign for Auldhouse. After 800 m the hamlet of Auldhouse is reached. This sleepy little hamlet has an attractive old world pub called the Auldhouse Inn, which has been the scene of many television productions.

At Auldhouse turn left past Auldhouse Primary School and carry on following the signs for East Kilbride. Continue along this undulating road for almost 1.2 km, at which point turn left. After 400 m turn left again. After a further 1.2 km turn right on to the road which is signed for Jackton. After 1.6 km a crossroads is reached. Turn right opposite the road which is signed for North and South Allerton. This is now the road which you left the bounds of East Kilbride at the beginning of the route, so follow the same route, in reverse, back to Hairmyres Station.

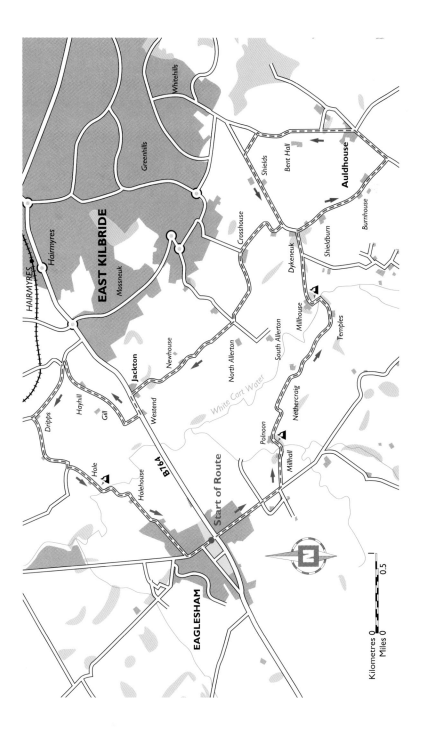

EAGLESHAM TO JACKTON

Eaglesham is a village with a very long history. It was the original home of the Montgomeries, Anglo-Norman knights, who had been granted land by Walter Fitzalan in these parts. Sir Hugh Montgomerie was later to serve Scotland so valiantly at the Battle of Otterburn (Chevy Chase) in 1388. There is no trace of the Montgomeries' castle left at Eaglesham, for it was considered to be a ruin even in the 18th century.

The village lies at the edge of the lonely moorlands which figured so greatly in Covenanting times with its network of remote almost hidden paths. It was here that, after a conventicle, the Covenanters could slide into the moorland mists away from the bloody attentions of Graham of Claverhouse, Grierson of Lagg and Turner, with their hellish crew of Dragoons, who scoured these parts in murderous pursuit.

The village under went great changes in 1769 when the 10th Earl of Eglinton had the old village demolished and had a new planned village built in its place. The new village was constructed in the form of a letter 'A' and is a striking example of Scottish domestic architecture of the time. When the village

INFORMATION

Distance: 14.5 km (9 miles), circular route.

Map: OS Landranger, sheet 64.

Start and finish: Gilmour Street, Eaglesham.

Terrain: Fairly flat with undulating stretches.

Refreshments: Various places in Eaglesham and the Auldhouse Inn, Auldhouse.

Old Parish Church, Eaglesham.

was built the houses had thatched roofs but these have all been replaced by slate. The two streets that form the 'A' are Polnoon Street and Montgomerie Street and, with the large common between, the shape is still clearly visible on a map. Today, this extremely pleasant village, with its 18th-century coaching inn, the Eglinton Arms, has been listed by the Secretary of State for Scotland as being of architectural and

Eglinton Arms, Eaglesham.

historical interest and has become a Conservation Area with most of the buildings having been refurbished.

Leave Eaglesham by Strathaven Road and after almost 800 m turn left at the junction signposted for Strathaven. This road carries on downhill and over the bridge which spans the Ardoch Burn, a tributary of the White Cart Water. Then along the generally undulating road for almost 3.2 km to another bridge, which this time spans the upper reaches of the White Cart Water itself. Almost immediately beyond this a short but fairly steep hill has to be climbed before reaching the next junction 800 m beyond. Here turn right at this 3-way junction and commence uphill again for a short distance through the pleasant farming countryside of Craigend and Harelaw farms, continue along the road bounded by high hedges to the next road junction. Here turn right and follow the Strathaven Road uphill. After 1.6 km carry straight on past a road on the right and take the next junction on the left and carry on for just over 800 m to the hamlet of Auldhouse.

As in Route 18, at Auldhouse turn left past Auldhouse Primary School and carry on following signs for East Kilbride along this undulating road for almost 1.2 km, at which point turn left. After 400 m turn left again. After a further 1.2 km turn right on to the road which is signed for Jackton. Carry along this road to Jackton, where it joins the B764, and turn left. After only a few hundred metres turn right into the very small Hayhill Road. Take care making this manoeuvre, for the B764 is, very often, busy with traffic.

Once on the 3 m-wide Hayhill Road the route becomes very quiet again and after 1.6 km turn left. This road winds gently uphill for about 800 m to the next junction, at which point turn left. About 800 m further on take the left fork and continue to a ford which crosses the White Cart Water once again. After the ford has been crossed, the road begins to climb quite steeply up to the beginning of Eaglesham entering the village at Holehouse Road, at the top of which it joins Gilmour Street.

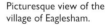

Picturesque view of the village of Eaglesham.

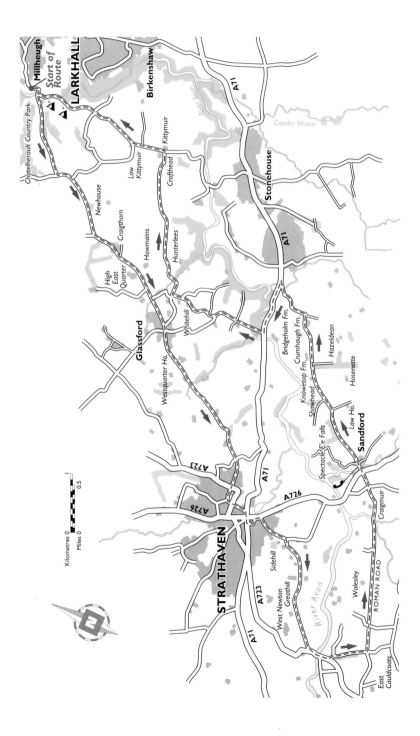

LARKHALL TO STRATHAVEN

This route starts from the car park at the bottom of Millheugh. Turn right uphill. The road winds round past the Applebank Inn to a bridge which crosses the Avon Water. (It is worth noting at this point that once the bridge has been crossed, there is a road off to the right that provides access into Chatelherault Country Park, its riverside paths forming a direct off-road link to Strathclyde Park. Although it may be permitted to cycle along these paths, there are areas where it is not conducive to cycling because in some places the path is very muddy and there are several sets of steps to negotiate.)

At the east end of the bridge carry straight on uphill fairly steeply for a short distance, then the hill continues its ascent less steeply for another 800 m. At a T-junction turn left and carry on along this fairly flat road for 1.6 km, at which point it starts to rise again quite steeply for a short distance. Pause here for a while and look back over the panoramic view of Lanarkshire. After just over 4.8 km the road comes into Glassford at the roundabout at Jackson Street. Here turn right into Millar Street.

The small village of Glassford, which is set amongst rich agricultural land, has for many hundreds of years had its roots in farming, although in the 18th-century it became a centre for hand-loom weaving.

The resolve of the Covenant was strong here, and many men fought at Bothwell Bridge and Drumclog to protect their faith. At the ruins of St Ninian's Parish Church there is a memorial to William Gordon of Earlston, who was shot by a troop of Dragoons while on his way to Bothwell Brig on 22 June 1679.

At the end of Millar Street the road continues on downhill to Strathaven,

INFORMATION

Distance: 28.1 km (17.5 miles), circular route.

Map: OS Landranger, sheets 64 and 71.

Start and finish: Larkhall car park, at the bottom of Millheugh, at the south side of the roundabout.

Terrain: mainly undulating with short stretches of steep hills.

Refreshments: Various places in Larkhall and Strathaven.

Cyclists in Strathaven.

arriving in the town at Commercial Road. Turn left into North Street, which joins Castle Street. At the end of this is a multiple junction. Here turn left into Todshill Street. After passing Station Road turn right into Newton Road, which takes you out of Strathaven again. At the next junction fork right and continue downhill for about 1.5 km to the 'Give Way' sign at the junction with the A723. Here turn left across the bridge, which spans the Avon Water. Join this A-class road, which never seems to be busy, for a little over 400 m to where a minor road goes off to the left. Take this road as it winds its way uphill fairly steeply in places until it joins the Roman road at a crossroads 800 m further on. Here turn left and follow this typical Roman road, which is straight but undulating, for 2.4 km. At this point, maps of the area suggest that the Roman road would have continued in a straight line while the modern road meanders around for another 800 m before it joins the A726. The route crosses this main road and continues on the minor road on the other side into Sandford.

The Kype Water.

Sandford is a pleasant little village, with the Kype Water flowing past it and its rows of single-storey cottages with their gardens ablaze with colour in the summer time. It has recently been given the status of a conservation village. Close to the village is located the famous local beauty spot known as the Spectacle E'e Falls. This beautiful waterfall took its name from a local tale of love and revenge. It is said that in the 18th century the miller of Overhall Mill had a beautiful daughter who was loved by a local Sandford lad, but the miller would not allow his daughter to have anything to do with him. One night, out of spite, the lad climbed on to the thatched roof of the mill and fixed a pair of spectacles to the thatch.

The next day when the sun rose the spectacles set fire to the roof. The local people saw from the surrounding fields that the mill was ablaze, but by the time they got to it and put the fire out only the four walls remained. When the mill was rebuilt it was henceforth known as the Spectacle E'e Mill and the, close-by, falls known as the Spectacle E'e Falls.

Carrying on from Sandford the road continues uphill steadily for 800 m. At this point there is a wooden signpost pointing out a right of way to Tweedy Hill, which also goes to the Spectacle E'e Falls.

The road continues undulating fairly steeply up and down to where it joins the A71, 3 km further on. Here turn left on to this main road and carry along it for a little less than 800 m and turn right on to the Glassford Road. Continue over Glassford Bridge, which spans the Avon Water, where the road begins to climb again. The climb is constant for 2 km, sometimes gradual and sometimes steep, until it reaches a crossroads. Just before this crossroads is located the ruins of the old St Ninian's Parish Church. Turn right at the crossroads and follow this road for 2.4 km to where a T-junction is reached and here turn left. Continue down this road for 400 m to another T-junction at Low Kittymuir Farm and turn right following the sign for Larkhall.

Ruins at Spectacle E'e Mill.

This minor road passes under a dismantled railway before beginning its descent back down to Millheugh. A word of warning: take care not to go too fast down the steep hill, which at times has a gradient of 1 in 7, for there are corners to negotiate. This road ends at the eastern end of the bridge over the Avon Water. Just cross this bridge again and within 300 m is the place where this route began, at the car park at the bottom of Millheugh.

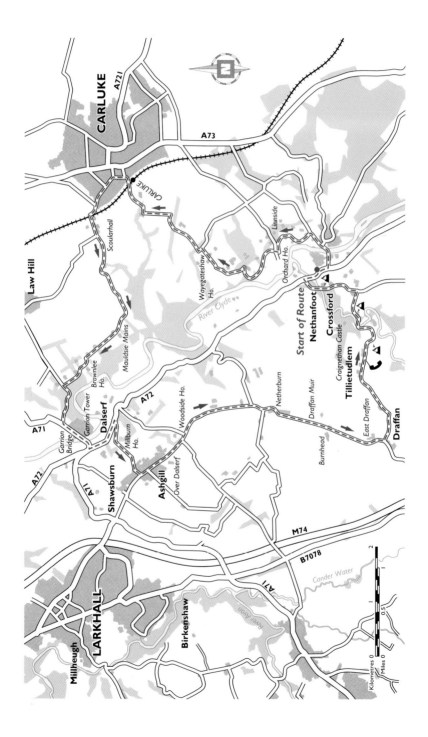

CROSSFORD TO CARLUKE

From the public car park at Crossford turn left on to the A72 for about 100 m then turn left on to the B7066 Braidwood Road and carry on across the stone bridge that spans the River Clyde. On the other side on the right is the Clyde Valley Country Estate, where there are many attractions to interest the visitor, including a Narrow Gauge Railway, Birds of Prey Centre, Pony Trekking Centre and also a cafeteria. Continue along the B7055 for less than 800 m where the first steep incline is located, but this is only about 200 m long. After this incline turn left on to the unclassified road signed for Waygateshaw. After 1.6 km on this pleasant road it starts to climb again at various gradients for 1.6 km. Some of these gradients are very steep indeed, but the very steep gradients tend to be over short distances.

At the top of this hill is a road junction. Turn left and continue along this road for about 800 m to the

INFORMATION

Distance: 28.1 km (17.5 miles), circular route.

Map: OS Landranger, sheets 65 and 72.

Start and finish: Crossford public car park.

Terrain: Undulating with stretches of very steep hills. Not suitable for inexperienced or unfit cyclists.

Refreshments: Various places in Crossford and Carluke.

junction with an even more minor road. Down this minor road at Milton Head was the birthplace of Major General William Roy of the Royal Engineers. Born in 1726, he is best known for his preparation of the map of mainland Scotland known as the Duke of

Footbridge over the river Clyde at Crossford.

Minature railway at
Crossford station.

Cumberland's Map, which can be seen in the British Museum in London. This map was the forerunner of the series of Ordnance Survey maps, which today are such a valuable asset to those wishing to venture into the countryside. He is also known for his work on the subject of the Roman occupation of Britain.

Carry on past this minor road to the next junction a few hundred metres further on and turn left. Follow this road over Jocks Burn, after which Carluke Railway Station is soon reached on the outskirts of the town.

Follow this road, which is Station Road, for a few hundred metres to Kirkton Avenue and turn left. If you are in need of refreshment then carry straight on to the end of this road and the centre of Carluke.

At the end of Kirkton Avenue turn left down Clyde Street to the roundabout and then carry straight on. Although this is only a C-class road it can be quite busy, but not busy enough to concern the cyclist. Carry on all the way downhill for 4 km, which is almost completely effortless and a very exhilarating experience, to the junction with the B7011. Here turn left and once again wind downhill to the junction with the A71, 800 m further on. Turn left on to the A71 to cross the beautiful River Clyde at Garrion Bridge.

At the crossroads at the west side of Garrion Bridge turn left and follow the A72 for 800 m to Dalserf. Here turn right on to a minor road. This is an awkward junction which turns back on itself. I therefore recommend that you dismount and re-mount when you are safely on the minor road. (At this point it is possible to foreshorten this cycle run, thus avoiding the most severe hill contained within the route. This is done by continuing south along the A72 to Crossford, which reduces this route to 17.7 km and gives the choice of doing the second part another time. A word of warning: this road can be very busy particularly at weekends.)

Opposite this road is a little road which makes its way down to the tiny hamlet of Dalserf, where at the end of its row of pretty cottages stands the beautiful and historic Dalserf Parish Church, founded in 1655. It is

here that John Macmillan (1669–1753) is buried. As the words on his monument say, he was the Covenanter of Covenanters. After being ordained in 1701 he joined the Cameronian movement, which was founded by Richard Cameron, who was known as

Author taking the route through a farmyard at Tillietudlum.

the Lion of the Covenant. Macmillan led the movement after Cameron's death, rejecting the settlement of the church and vowing to continue to fight for the right of the Covenant. The Cameronian movement retained its identity and finally was instrumental in setting up the Free Church of Scotland in 1876. The Cameronian Regiment was also raised from this group.

This road winds uphill very steeply at first then less steeply and after 800 m the top of this hill is reached. Here the view over the Clyde Valley is magnificent. Soon this road comes into the small village of Ashgill at Millburn Road. Here if you turn right it is less than 3.2 km into the heart of Larkhall.

Our route is to the left at this junction. Follow this road, through Netherburn, for 4.8 km. Here turn left at the road junction signed for Craignethan Castle. As the road turns east there are panoramic views over the Clyde Valley and the hills to the south of Lanarkshire. At the next junction turn left, still following signs for Craignethan Castle. The road then passes through the tiny hamlet of Tillietudlem, at the end of which is the entrance to Craignethan Castle.

Craignethan Castle was built in the 1530s for Sir James Hamilton. It was the last of the fortress residences to be built in Scotland. From its position high on top a hill, protected on three sides by a steep escarpment, around which the Water of Nethan still meanders, it should have been an impenetrable fortress. This however was not the case; for the castle was sacked and laid waste before the end of the 16th century. Craignethan Castle is Sir Walter Scott's Tillietudlem Castle in *Old Mortality*.

Just after passing this entrance the road begins to descend at a gradient of 12 per cent, which is clearly signed at the top of the hill. Take care cycling down this hill for there are some double bends to contend with en route, so keep the speed down. Perhaps even walk! At the bottom of this hill the road passes through a farmyard and then over a bridge spanning

A Golden Eagle at the Bird of Prey Centre.

the River Nethan. At this point there is a good view of Craignethan Castle over to the left. Here the opposite of the old proverb is true, for in this case what comes down must go up. The road rises as steeply, for 800 m, back uphill as it previously descended. Once again it may be advisable to walk this stretch. At the end of this hill a road junction is reached, here turn left and commence the descent down to Crossford. Care should also be taken on this descent with an effort being made to keep down the speed. At the bottom of this hill turn right on to the A72 at the Tillietudlem Hotel and commence along this road for a few hundred metres back to the car park.

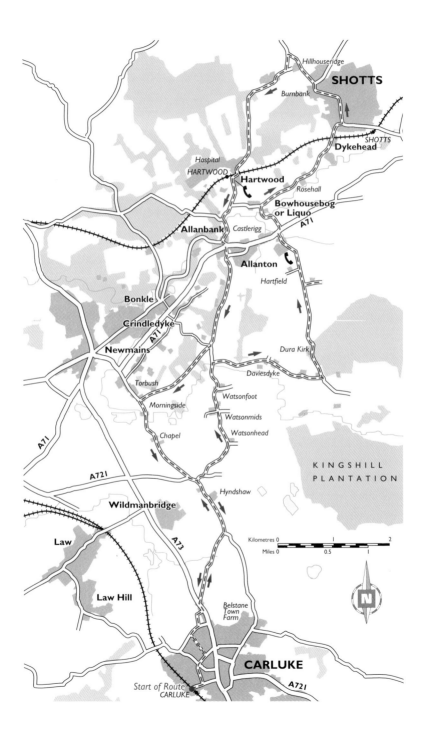

SHOTTS

Hillhouseridge

Burnbank

SHOTTS

Dykehead

Hospital
HARTWOOD

Hartwood

Rosehall

Bowhousebog
or Liquo

A71

Allanbank Castlerigg

Allanton

Hartfield

Bonkle

Crindledyke

A71

Newmains

Dura Kirk

Daviesdyke

Torbush

Watsonfoot

Morningside

Watsonmids

Chapel

Watsonhead

A71

KINGSHILL
PLANTATION

A721

Hyndshaw

Wildmanbridge

A73

Law

Kilometres 0   1   2
Miles 0   0.5   1

Law Hill

N

Belstane
Town
Farm

CARLUKE

Start of Route
CARLUKE

A721

CARLUKE TO SHOTTS

The parish of Carluke was granted the status of Burgh of Barony, by King Charles II in 1662, in favour of Captain Walter Lochart of Kirktoune. However, the town that is seen today did not come into being until later.

On leaving the station car park turn right on to Station Road and follow this for a few hundred metres and turn left into Kirkton Avenue. At the end of this, cross Clyde Street into Kirk Street then right into Kirk Road. Follow this road to the junction with Holm Street and turn left into Holm Street. At the junction with Douglas Street, Holm Street ends but on the opposite side of the road a footpath continues. This is what is left of Old Wishaw Road. Carry on down this footpath, for it is permitted to cycle here, to Weighhouse Road and turn right. Take the first on the left into Bothwell Road and then take the third on the right into Stirling Road. Stirling Road is only a few metres long, at the end of which there is another footpath leading to Airdrie Road. This time the cyclist will have to dismount for the few metres on this footpath. Cross over the busy Airdrie Road, which is the A73, into Castlehill Road. The route now continues along this road, into the countryside, for 1.5 km to a road junction. At this point turn left and continue along this road, which has a short but steep uphill stretch. Turn right at the next junction, which has a sign saying 'weight limit 10T ½ mile ahead'.

It is easy to see from the splendid views, as far as the Campsie Fells, that this area is generally very high, about 200 m above sea level in fact. This quiet unclassified road meanders through picturesque agricultural land and passes large affluent farm houses at regular intervals. After passing under a disused railway bridge, there is another road junction 2.4 km further on. Here turn right and wind slowly uphill for 400 m. In fact within this stretch there are a few hills to contend with, none of them being particularly long

INFORMATION

Distance: 30.5 km (19 miles), circular route.

Map: OS Landranger, sheets 65 and 72.

Start and finish: Carluke Railway Station.

Terrain: Undulating with long flat stretches.

Refreshments: Various places in Carluke and Shotts.

Ruins of Dura Kirk.

or steep. At the next junction turn left and continue past the forest known as Kingshill Plantation and the ruins of Dura Kirk.

In 1740 a previous church known as the Moor Kirk of Cambusnethan was built on this site, but this heather-roofed structure was replaced by the present building in 1780. However, this church fell into disrepair when the congregation moved to Bonkle, a few miles to the north, in 1843.

From here the surrounding countryside changes to that of open moorland. There are considerable signs of quarrying with a few spoil heaps dotted around, although the ambiance of the area is not unpleasant. Soon begins the descent into the village of Allanton, where the A71 is reached. Cross this busy road, and 200 m to the right is situated another minor road along which the route continues.

Descend down this pretty little road for 800 m to the next road junction and turn right. If one turns left at this point however, and carries along this road for less than 800 m and turns left at the T-junction, joining up with the route again further on, this foreshortens the route by under 6.4 km. This shorter route is for the most part easy cycling. Continuing on along the route, after turning right the road begins to ascend towards Shotts with short stretches of fairly steep gradients to contend with from time to time. On entering Shotts this road becomes Rosehall Road, at the end of which it joins Shottskirk Road and Station Road. (Turn right down Station Road, if you want to go to the railway station.) Turn left into Shottskirk Road passing two streets on the left before coming to a 4-way junction. Here Shottskirk Road continues on the left out of

Shotts and so does the route passing, on the way, the headquarters of the Central Scottish Countryside Trust. Turn left at the T-junction following the sign for Hartwood. After a short uphill stretch this road descends down for almost 2.4 km, passing Murdostoun Forest, into Hartwood with its large hospital. Once through this little village the short cut referred to earlier rejoins the main route. It may also be useful to note that Hartwood has a railway station with a park and ride facility.

Then 200 m past where the short cut merges is another junction. Here carry straight on and after a further few hundred metres a T-junction is reached at Allanbank. Turn left and within a very short distance the A71 is once more reached. At this point dismount and cross this road to reach a footpath located on the other side. Turn right, commence up this footpath and after 100 m it joins a road end called Mill Road. Very soon Mill Road comes to a T-junction, at which point veer right (do not turn hard right) and on out of the village. This little manoeuvre saves a 800 m detour through Allanton. (The alternative route through Allanton is: turn left along the A71 for 200 m or so and then turn right into Coltness Avenue and follow this uphill and out of the village.) Follow this road for about 1.5 km to a 4-way junction. Here veer to the right (once again do not turn hard right). Carry along this road for 1.6 km to Morningside and turn left at a T-junction there. Once out of this tiny hamlet the road begins to climb sometimes fairly steeply for 800 m when it levels out once again. A little further on, the road which was used on the first leg of the journey is passed on the left. Carry on for a further 800 m, now retracing the route already travelled upon to the next junction where a right turn is made. From here retrace this route back for 1.2 km, to where it joins the A72. Then carry on using the reverse of the route through Carluke to the railway station.

View over Shotts with the Pentland Hills in the background.

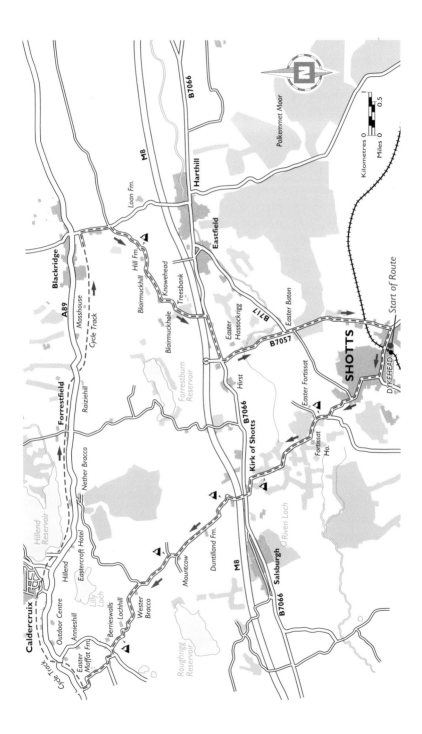

SHOTTS TO BLACKRIDGE

From Shotts Railway Station turn left and continue along Station Road, which after passing through the town centre becomes Shottskirk Road. Carry on uphill on Shottskirk Road, passing two streets on the left before coming to a 4-way junction. Here Shottskirk Road continues on the left out of Shotts, and so does the route. Turn right at the T-junction following the sign for Caldercruix. After passing the perimeter fence of HM Prison Shotts, the road begins to climb uphill, sometimes steeply for short distances, for 1.6 km until the summit, at 300 m above sea level, is reached. On this incline after about 800 m is the Fortissat Stone or Covenanters' Stone, which is clearly visible as it protrudes out on to the road. This stone was used as a meeting place for conventicles by 40 Covenanters from Shotts parish. At the top of this hill, as a treat for the effort made to get up, there is a splendid view over West Lanarkshire and beyond.

INFORMATION

Distance: 32.2 km (20 miles), circular route.

Map: OS Landranger, sheet 65.

Start and finish: Shotts Railway Station car park.

Terrain: Mainly undulating with short stretches of fairly steep hills.

Refreshments: Various places in, Shotts, Plains, Caldercruix and Blackridge.

Fortisat, or Covenanters Stone near Shotts.

After 800 m the road begins to climb again for a short distance before making its descent down to the Kirk o Shotts. (This beautiful old parish church was built at the beginning of the 19th century and stands in a most imposing position.) A few hundred metres past the church the junction with the B7086 is reached. Here turn right, then almost immediately left and continue across the bridge, which spans the M8 motorway.

After crossing the motorway the road climbs steeply for 500 m to where once more there is another incredible panoramic view all the way to Glasgow and beyond.

From here also there is a good view of Roughrigg Reservoir, a short distance to the west. In the next 2.4 km the road is very undulating climbing gradually with 3 short expanses of steep incline interspersed with short downhill stretches until finally it reaches the summit. Almost at the top of this hill is located the Blackhill Transmitter, which, with its near neighbour, Kirk o Shotts, to the east, beams television signals to Central Scotland.

The road then descends for a little over 1.5 km to where a T-junction is located, at which turn left. After only 200 m, at the next junction, turn right into Brownieside Road and commence downhill once again. This road becomes Station Road Plains, where the Glasgow to Edinburgh cycle route bisects.

Turn right here on to the Glasgow to Edinburgh cycle track and follow it for the next 12.9 km to Blackridge. Since this cycle route is built on the disused railway solum of the Glasgow to Bathgate railway, and is well defined and signed along its length, it is not necessary to describe the route in detail. I will, however, point out the places of interest along the way.

The Calor Man near Hillend Reservoir.

After 3.2 km Hillend Reservoir is reached. This is a

particularly attractive area with a wooded backdrop on the other side of the loch. It is used by many anglers, who can be seen sitting on the banks, rod in hand, fishing at all times of the day during both summer and winter. This part of the cycleway is also used by many people enjoying a walk along the loch side.

Also along this stretch there are 2 sculptures: the first called *Calorman* depicts a fisherman with rod and line and the second called *Bedrock Bicycle* is, as its name suggests, a bicycle of gigantic proportions. Both of these were constructed from an idea by Dave Holliday, formerly of Sustrans.

Once Hillend Reservoir is passed, it is about 10 km along this pleasant cycle path, from North Lanarkshire into West Lothian, to Blackridge. At the end of the cycle path, continue along a road for a few hundred metres to a T-junction. Here turn right and continue uphill, on the B718 out of Blackridge. A hundred metres past the village there is a minor road off to the right. Follow this very pleasant little road for about 3 km as it climbs south-west, sometimes steeply, towards the M8 motorway. After passing under the motorway the T-junction with the B7066 is reached. Turn right and follow this road for just over 1 km to the next junction, at which point turn left on to the B7057. Now follow this road for about 3 km to a roundabout. Here turn right into Shotts, where after a short distance Shotts Railway Station is reached.

The Bedrock Bicycle near Hillend reservoir.

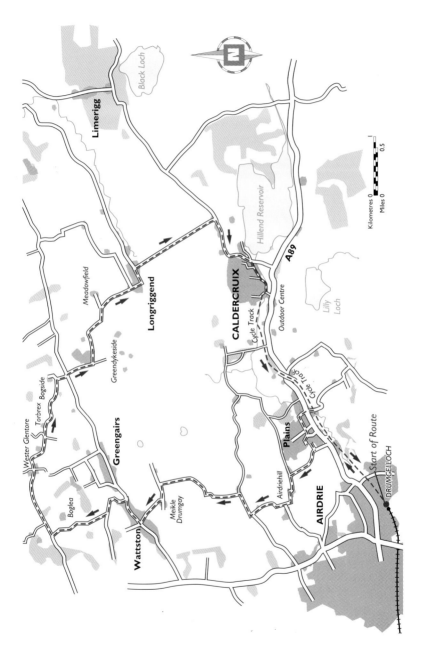

AIRDRIE TO LONGRIGGEND

I n the words of the local song:
Airdrie's a rer wee toon so it is, so it is
Airdrie's a rer wee toon
It's better than Greenock, it's better than Troon,
Some people say it's better than Dunoon.

(Sung to the tune of: 'Who were you with last night, under the pale moonlight')

It is obvious that Airdrieonians have a certain pride in where they come from, and so they should have for in the year of writing this book (1995) Airdrie Football Club were runners-up in the Scottish Cup – a feat which they have achieved twice thus far in this decade. Alas however, on both occasions, they were beaten in the final, first by Glasgow Rangers and then by Glasgow Celtic. But their pride extends to more than football, for Airdrie and its near neighbour Coatbridge are vibrant places with a very special and distinctive character.

In 1996 the Glasgow to Edinburgh cycle route is due to be completed, and this will run through both Coatbridge and Airdrie from end to end.

The first part of this route from Drumgelloch Station to Plains is about 3 km long and uses the already opened part of this cycle route. Indeed on the return journey it also uses it from Caldercruix back to Drumgelloch Station. At Station Road, which bisects the cycle path, turn left and after about a hundred metres the junction with Main Road, which is also the A89, is reached. Cross this road into Northburn Street then left into Jarvie Street. Follow Jarvie Street around until it joins Wallace Street and turn left. At the next junction turn right into Bruce Street and then take the next street on the left, which is Annieshill View. At the end of this turn right into Meadowhead Road and on out of Plains.

This minor road winds uphill, sometimes steeply, for 800 m. This is the most severe climb that will be encountered on this route. At the top of this hill turn

INFORMATION

Distance: 26.5 km (16.5 miles), circular route.

Map: OS Landranger, sheets 64 and 65.

Start and finish: Drumgelloch Railway Station car park.

Terrain: Mainly undulating with fairly flat stretches.

Refreshments: Various places in Plains and Caldercruix.

left. Follow this road, passing 2 junctions on the left, for about 2.4 km to a 3-way junction and turn left into Darngavil Road. Continue along this road for another 2.4 km into Wattston. I confess that the scenery adjacent to this road, at the moment, is not very attractive, but the land is being rehabilitated by Central Scottish Countryside Trust. However, it is worthwhile tolerating this temporary blot because after Wattston the scenery improves dramatically.

Once Wattston is reached turn right on to the B803 in the direction of Greengairs. Travel through the village

A view over Hillend reservoir.

A fisherman at Hillend Loch.

for 400 m and then turn left on to a road known as Cameron Road. (This is the first on the left after the village has been passed.) Carry on around this road for 800 m or so and take the road off to the right known as Brackenknowe Road. Now, as I promised, the scenery is much better, with fine views across to Cumbernauld and the Kilsyth Hills beyond. The only warning I should give is that the road surface on this minor road is bad, so care should be taken here.

At the end of this road turn right and follow this now extremely pleasant minor road, which I must say reminded me in places of France, with the trees on both sides, although they are not cedars. After 800 m the road continues past roads on the right and the left, then starts to climb in steps sometimes quite steeply, for short distances, for another 800 m.

Another junction with the B803 is reached 1.6 km further on. Here turn left and within a few metres right again following the road signed for Longriggend Remand Centre. The road commences uphill, which includes 100 m of very steep climb, before passing the Remand Centre, after which it levels off for 800 m. It starts to climb again gradually for a few hundred metres to where a road junction is reached. Here turn right following the road on to the small hamlet of Longriggend. Once over the humped-back railway bridge the road turns at right angles, now called Main Street, through the small village. After 250 m the junction with Telegraph Road is reached. Turn right on to Telegraph Road and commence past the peat fields on either side to the junction with the B825. Carry on downhill to Caldercruix and turn right into the village at Main Street. Commence along Main Street and over the old railway bridge, which now passes over the Glasgow to Edinburgh cycle track. Continue to the bottom of this street where Longriggend and Meadowfield Church are located. Here on the west side of the church the access to the cycle track is found. From here carry on to the cycle track and continue back in a westerly direction, 4.8 km, to Drumgelloch Station.

Tree lined road - A pleasure to cycle.

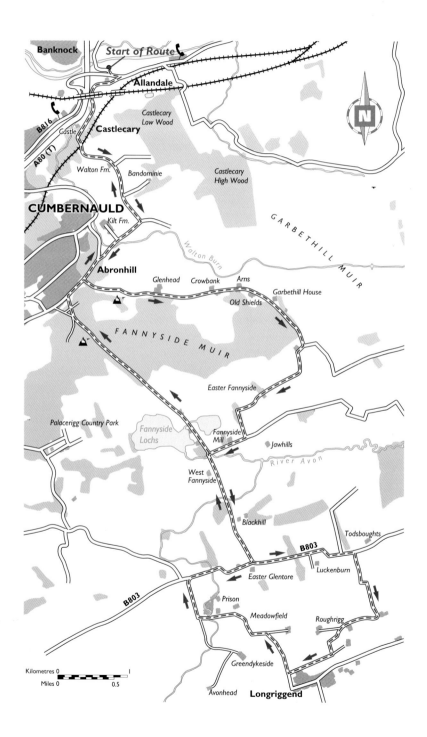

CASTLECARY TO LONGRIGGEND

Castle Cary was built in 1473 by the Livingston family and is still standing today. Cary meaning fort from the old word 'caer', Castle Cary therefore means the 'castle of the fort'. The original fort was Roman, and the castle was built re-using its stone.

The route begins at the Forth and Clyde Canal at Castlecary. Commence up the road from the canal bank and turn left on to the A80 access road and continue on to the junction with B816. Turn right and almost immediately turn left on to Walton Road. This road winds round and under the viaduct which carries the main Glasgow to Edinburgh railway high above. The road then begins to ascend fairly gradually for 1.6 km passing Castle Cary. There are good views over Cumbernauld and the hills beyond from this

INFORMATION

Distance: 28.9 km (18 miles), circular route.

Map: OS Landranger, sheets 64 and 65.

Start and finish: Adjacent to the canal at Castlecary. If driving to the beginning of this route at Castlecary, commence along the B816 in the direction of Bonnybridge and then turn into the access road for the A80 in the direction of Glasgow. Half way down this access road the canal access road is located on the right. There is no formal car park here but the road is broad and there is room for a few cars to park quite comfortably.

Terrain: Fairly flat with 2 long gradual hills.

Refreshments: 1.6 km (1 mile) further east from Castlecary there is a restaurant and bar called Underwood Lockhouse.

Top; The beginning of the route at Castlecary on the Forth and Clyde canal.

Bottom:Underwood lockhouse near Castlecary.

road. After another 1.2 km the road begins to wind uphill once again for a short distance to where a T-junction is reached. Here turn left on to a fine modern road, but within only a few hundred metres turn left on to the road which is signed for Arns. This road immediately begins to ascend fairly gradually once again for a short distance. The road continues almost flat and dead straight for 1.6 km and then begins to gradually wind uphill again for a short distance past the small cluster of houses which is Arns. This little minor road is a perfect road for cycling. On now past a radar mast, 400 m after which a T-junction is reached, where a right turn is made.

On now for 1.2 km to where the road passes straight through the yard of Easter Fannyside Farm. Take care here for there is a road hump across the road in this farmyard but this should not be of particular harm to the cyclist. The countryside here is very pleasant with Fannyside Lochs visible on the right. Soon afterwards turn right and after passing Fannyside Mill carry on to a T-junction and turn left. There is now another very straight stretch of road, which continues, on the rise, for 1.6 km to where it joins the B803. Here turn left and commence gradually uphill from time to time for 1.6 km. At the point where a sign showing a speed camera is located, turn right on to another minor road.

Follow this picturesque country road for 3.2 km, as it meanders around a few bends and uphill gradually to where it joins the Longriggend Road, just at the beginning of the village itself. However, unless a shop is required, turn right and head away from Longriggend. After 2 km the road rises steeply for 200 m as it passes Longriggend Remand Centre before descending to the B803 once again. Here turn right and continue along the B803 for 1.2 km to the road junction where the B803 was joined some 8 km before.

Turn left back on to this minor road once again but this time carry straight on at the next junction. This road now passes between Fannyside Lochs with a boat yard on the left. The land which borders the road in

Castle Cary.

this vicinity is full of peat. After 1.5 km the road then begins to descend through the woods of Fannyside Muir, towards Cumbernauld.

Just before entering Cumbernauld the descent becomes steep so take care here not to gather too much speed. Soon a T-junction is reached. Here turn right following the sign for Castlecary. After 800 m, passing en route the Arns Road once again, there is the junction of the road which was used for the first leg of this route. Turn right on to this road where it is signed for Castlecary and retrace this route back to the Forth and Clyde Canal.

Cyclists using the canal towpath

INDEX

HMSO Bookshops
71 Lothian Road, Edinburgh EH3 9AZ
0131-228 4181 Fax 0131-229 2734
49 High Holborn, London WC1V 6HB
(counter service only)
0171-873 0011 Fax 0171-831 1326
68–69 Bull Street, Birmingham B4 6AD
0121-236 9696 Fax 0121-236 9699
33 Wine Street, Bristol BS1 2BQ
0117 9264306 Fax 0117 9294515
9-21 Princess Street, Manchester M60 8AS
0161-834 7201 Fax 0161-833 0634
16 Arthur Street, Belfast BT1 4GD
01232 238451 Fax 01232 235401
The HMSO Oriel Bookshop, The Friary, Cardiff
CF1 4AA
01222 395548 Fax 01222 384347

HMSO publications are available from:

HMSO Publications Centre
(Mail, fax and telephone orders only)
PO Box 276, London SW8 5DT
Telephone orders 0171-873 9090
General enquiries 0171-873 0011
(queuing system in operation for both numbers)
Fax orders 0171-873 8200

HMSO's Accredited Agents
(see Yellow Pages)

and through good booksellers